顶上英语双语分级阅读系

孙健总主编

SAT阅读进阶攻略

周日进 编著

topschool

中国人民大学出版社

·北京·

推荐序

SAT，申请美国高排名本科院校需要参考的考试之一。我是 2004 年第一次接触，当时刚刚备考完美国研究生考试 GRE，本以为 SAT 会比 GRE 简单很多，就像中国的高考英语相较于研究生英语会简单很多一样。做完一套试卷后，感觉很受打击，因为以 GRE 水平的英文去看 SAT，尤其是阅读部分，还是有很吃力的感觉。

后来分析了一下原因，大致有以下几点：

(1) SAT 考查的不是知识（Knowledge），而是思维（Reasoning）。

(2) SAT 不像 TOEFL 这类为非母语学生专门设计的语言考试，而是以美国高中生应该具备的分析理解和语言能力为出发点的。

(3) SAT 对于英语基本能力，比如词汇和语法的要求，不是表面的数量和定义，而是运用和理解。

在接触 SAT 之前，包括我在内的大部分中国学生，都没有系统、全面接触过 SAT。所以初次学习 SAT 会有很多的不适应感和挫折感。

从 2016 年开始，最新版的 SAT 改革完成并推出执行。这一版的 SAT，尤其是阅读部分，保留了 SAT 一以贯之的对分析理解和推理思考能力的考查。对词汇的要求，完全取消了以数量制胜的题目类型，转而考查基于上下文分析理解。

经过多年对 SAT 的研究，基于对于各个分数段的 SAT 考生，尤其是中国学生的观察，笔者总结出一套备考思路体系，大致有以下几步。

(1) 开始备考 SAT 之前，务必掌握基础词汇和 SAT 核心词汇，基础词汇指的是托福及托福以下难度的词汇，数量大约是 8000—9000 个，SAT 核心词汇大约是 2500 个。

(2) 开始备考以后，首先不要盲目做题，不要"刷题"，而是要从阅读、语法和写作三个方面了解、理解并掌握 SAT 考试相关的知识体系，对于 SAT 数学，大部分中国学生都没有知识点的困难。

(3) 掌握了知识体系以后，再按照正确的方法进行练习和模拟考试，然后做知识点复习和巩固基础能力，主要是词汇的巩固。

《SAT 阅读进阶攻略》就是以 SAT 阅读文章分析为素材，系统、全面地介绍与 SAT 阅读学习相关的所有知识。这本书是我主持开发的"双语分级阅读系列"的 SAT 分册，与托福阅读、SSAT 阅读、中高考英语阅读等构成分级学习的阅读部分的指导图书。双语分级阅读与分级词汇学习、分级语法学习和分级口语学习一起，构成了英语分级学习方法论的指导丛书。

本书可以用于备考 SAT 阅读，也可以用来进行高级英语阅读能力的提升，帮助考生了解相关背景知识，比如美国历史、英美文学、西方哲学简史等。

希望学习者可以通过本书的学习，领悟到高级英语阅读的方法和理论，在 SAT 考出好成绩的同时，英语能力得到本质的提高。

孙健

2018 年 11 月 7 日

于荷兰阿姆斯特丹

序言

SAT 考试在 2016 年改革以后，阅读的题型和考查思路出现了较大的变化。以前的阅读是 critical reading（批判性阅读），现在是 evidence-based reading（证据性阅读）；以前的 SAT 中会出现很多生僻的单词，甚至专门设计了一种叫做句子填空的题型；现在的文章和题目中删除了很多这类生僻单词，阅读只有五篇长度相似的文章和题目；以前的阅读分成三个部分，现在的阅读就是第一部分，而且是时间最长的部分（65 分钟）。为了让备考 SAT 的考生能够更好地了解目前 SAT 的考查本质和提升阅读板块的能力，过去 6 个月，我利用工作之余的时间整理了这些年的授课和实战经验，按照不同的能力分类编著了这本 SAT 阅读参考资料。

我是从 2010 年开始教授托福 /ACT/SAT 阅读单项的；截至 2018 年，我参加过 14 次 SAT/ACT 的实际考试（爵禄街的新蒲岗考试考评局也成了我在香港最熟悉的地方），每次都获得了阅读满分或是高分的成绩。但是 SAT 阅读是大多数中国学生最难获得高分的单项，其原因无非在于：读不懂，做不对，做不完——分别对应的三种能力是文章理解能力、做题方法和整体阅读速度。而这三种能力又由很多个小方面构成，相互交织在一起，使得阅读的提高变成了缓慢而又艰难的过程。

那么，这本书就是将这些谜团一样的能力划分为不同的章节。从文章阅读和标记方法、段落的核心概括和重点把握、各类题型的突破方法以及历史类文章的长难句专题等方面入手，系统地提升大家实际阅读和做题时候的操作和思考方法。具体内容大家看一下目录也就清晰了。另外，为了让这本书看起来不要太厚，我们在最后一个章节——历史类重要文献与评析——只放了几篇文献，话题是涉及美国建国、政府制度、黑人和女权运动；如果想获得更多这类文献的学习资料，大家也可以联系我们获取。我的个人邮箱是 546558350@qq.com。

在本书的出版过程中，非常感谢顶上教育孙健老师的支持与关照，在留学培训界，孙老师是一位让我很尊敬的前辈；同时也感谢吕蕾老师的辛勤付出与审核。最后，感谢家人对我工作和写书的支持。

致谢

在本书编写过程中，黄卓明、薛淡、李帅、周可、桂林、陈美佳、黄双勤、王振军、郭浩、叶紫檀、刘姗姗、吴迪、周晓康、王业、张靖娴、陈志爽、张美容、吕依儒、贾红梅、杨志等也参与了资料收集及部分编写工作，在此一并感谢。

周日进

目 录

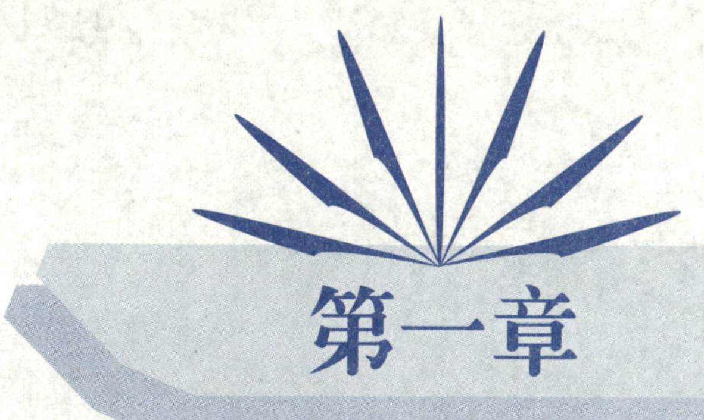

第一章

SAT 阅读介绍与常见备考问题

SAT 阅读部分概览

考试时间：65 分钟（含涂卡时间）。

文章数量：5 篇。其中 1 篇美国 / 世界文学、1 篇社会科学文章、1 篇美国 / 全球对话文献以及 2 篇自然科学文章。

每篇文章长度：500—750 个单词。

题量：52 题（每篇文章 10—11 题）。

阅读部分总分：400 分。

根据官方指南的讲解，阅读部分的题目归为三大类。

1. 信息观点类题

(1) 细节 / 推理题

要求考生在文章中找到作者清晰表达的意思或暗含的意思。通常考查作者直接清晰表达的信息时，题干中会出现“according to the passage”“states”“indicates”等类似表达；而考查作者暗含的信息时，题干中会出现“based on the passage”“it can be reasonably be inferred”“implies”等类似表达。

(2) 询证题

通常是询问考生从文章哪些行号可得到上题的答案（上下题询证）；少数情况下出现单个询证题，考查哪些行号支持题干的结论或信息。

(3) 核心观点 / 主旨题

通常题干中会出现“main idea”“theme”“central idea”“main point”等表达，考查考生对整篇文章或是部分段落的主要观点的概括。

(4) 关系识别题

考查对因果关系、类比 / 对比关系、时间顺序等各类关系的判定。

(5) 词汇题

考查某个单词 / 短语在文章语境中的准确意思。题干关键词为“the word...most nearly means...”。

2. 修辞题

(1) 语气题

考查单词 / 短语对文章的语气或语言风格的影响。

(2) 结构题

考查对文章结构的把握，通常题干中会出现“the main focus of the passage shift from...to...”。

（3）文章视角 / 立场题

比如小说的视角题（point of view）或者其他文章的立场题（stance）。

（4）目的题

要求考生不仅要理解句子 / 段落的意思，而且还需要知道句子 / 段落的作用；题干关键词通常为 “function” “serve to” “purpose”。

3. 语气题

（1）对比文章的关系题、求同题、求异题等

（2）图文结合题

考查文章和图表的关系。

本书后面章节会对以上重点题型进行详细分析和阐述。

SAT 备考常见问题

常见问题 1：SAT 考多少分才是不错的分数？

每个人对不错的分数的理解不一样，我们可以参考 SAT 官方在 2017 年发布的两个标准。

（1）SAT 大学和职业准备参照分（SAT College and Career Readiness Benchmarks）

阅读和文法是 480 分，数学是 530 分；也就是说，总分在 1010 以上就算是达到了大学的入学门槛，但这个分数对于中国学生来说肯定是太低了。

（2）官方统计的学生分数排名

其中 50% 这个百分比排位表对应的阅读和文法分数是 530 分，数学是 520 分。也就是说，如果一位学生的总分是 1050 分，就属于中等水平了。当然，这个分数在中国考生看来还是不理想的。

所以，具体多少分比较理想主要看个人的标准和目标。而根据官方发布的数据，只有前 5% 的考生能够达到 1400 +；大概有 6% 的考生在阅读和文法中取得了 700—800 分的成绩，阅读和文法是中国考生最有区别度和最有含金量的部分。

阅读、文法、数学部分的平均分分别是 270、260、260。如果按照中国学生的标准，如果阅读 270 分，阅读和文法总分应该在 550—580 分左右，数学按照 750 分来算，总分应该是 1300 分以上。高于这个分数对于申请才是比较有意义的。

常见问题 2：如果阅读部分想达到 300 分或 350 分，那么能错几题？

这个问题的本质是阅读答对题目和分数的对应换算问题。官方对于每次考试都会给出一个

分数转换表（raw score conversion table），而且转换表每次不完全一样，但是基本上一致。阅读如果想达到 300 分左右，容错个数大约为 12 个；阅读想达到 350 分，容错个数在 7 个左右。

常见问题 3：SAT 备考一般需要多久？

这个问题也是因人而异的，通常大部分考生备考周期在 6—15 个月。比较典型的备考方案是：

托福取得 90＋分数：SAT 基础段学习（获得 1350＋分）；

SAT 进阶段 / 强化段学习（获得 1450＋分）；

SAT 冲刺段学习（获得理想的高分）。

每个阶段的学习时间在 60 小时左右，如果每周投入 8 个小时学习，需要约 8 周时间。在寒暑假集中学习会获得更好的效果。

常见问题 4：SAT 如何报名？

SAT 统一在官网进行注册和报名：www.collegeboard.org。

目前，每年在北美地区有 3 月、5 月、6 月、8 月、10 月、11 月和 12 月共七次考试机会。而亚洲考试机会比北美少，目前只有每年的 3 月、5 月、10 月和 12 月可以进行 SAT 考试（6 月和 11 月可以进行 SAT Subject 考试）。

常见问题 5：应该使用哪些题目进行练习？

就练习的题目而言，最推荐的就是官方试题了。目前，官方试题分成两类。

（1）官方指南＋历年真题

最早的官方指南（Official Guide）有四套试题，然后 2017 年的版本又加入了四套真题（2016 年 5 月北美和亚洲的试题、2016 年 10 月北美试题以及 2017 年 1 月北美试题）。

（2）官方在可汗学院网站上发布的试题

https://www.khanacademy.org，大家可以登录网站，然后进入到 SAT 板块进行练习。

而对于其他试题，比如各个机构出版的模拟题，就真心不是特别推荐了，主要原因是文章的难度和题目的设计思路与官方试题存在一定的差异，甚至个别机构出的题目都有错误。

所以，大家基本上把官方试题全部理解和消化就已经很好。此外，题目不怕做第二遍甚至第三遍。如果你半年前做过某套试题，现在基本上已忘记题目和答案了。

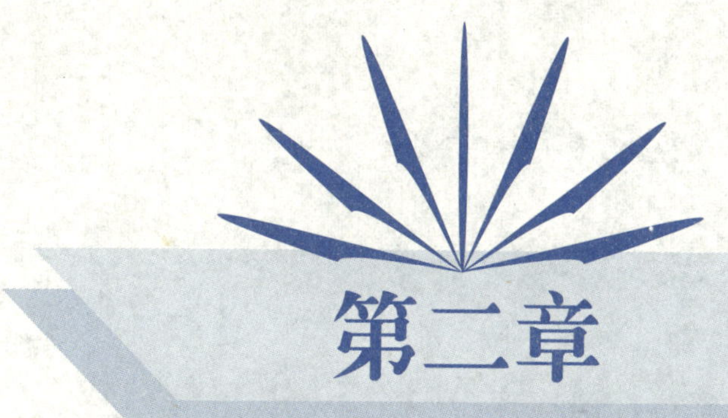

第二章

读文章，读什么？主旨结构题思考方法

本章主要介绍了三类题材文章的阅读时间分配、阅读方法和标记的重点。SAT 考试阅读部分一共 5 篇文章，其中有三篇是科学类（两篇科学类和一篇社会科学类）、一篇历史类以及一篇文学类。不同的文章时间分配和标记的重点不一样。根据阅读文章和做题所需的时间，通常我们按照以下策略进行分配（考试时间为 65 分钟，涂卡一般需要 5 分钟，每篇文章平均需要在 12 分钟左右完成）。

科学类文章：3—4 分钟读文章，7—8 分钟做题。

历史类文章：4—5 分钟读文章，7—8 分钟做题。

文学类文章：5—6 分钟读文章，6—7 分钟做题。

科学类文章

科学类文章的单句难度不是很大，行文思路通常也比较简单。在用 3—4 分钟读文章时候，需要重点标记以下内容。

1. 文章的话题（topic of the passage）。
2. 每段的段落概要（main idea of each paragraph）。
3. 出现的每个科学家名字（experts' names）。
4. 转折 / 对比的地方（transition and contrast）。

文章的话题通常会在首段引出，考生很容易寻找到。每段的段落概要可以说是科学类文章最重要的标记重点了。这里涉及大家概括段落的能力：如果段落概括得好，阅读速度会提升，理解也会更好；反之，不会概括的同学会发现读完整篇文章后想不起来文章讲了什么，最多只记得一些细枝末节，没有整体结构的概念。

标记科学家的名字主要是为了防止出题时候题干中出现而定位不到的情况；转折 / 对比的地方是任何文章都应该标记的重点，很大概率会出现试题。

因为 SAT 是纸质考试，所以大家在阅读时候一定要学会标记，建议大家养成画线和画圈的习惯。对于科学家名字进行画线，对于文章的话题、段落概要以及转折 / 对比的地方进行画圈。另外，如果一个段落没有直接出现概括性的句子，大家可以自行在空白处写上几个简单的单词或中文。

下面我们以官方指南上的一篇文章进行标记示范。

Questions 43–52 are based on the following passage and supplementary material.

This passage is adapted from Geoffrey Giller, "Long a Mystery, How 500-Meter-High Undersea Waves Form Is Revealed." ©2014 by *Scientific American*.

Some of the largest ocean waves in the world are nearly impossible to see. Unlike other large waves, these rollers, called internal waves, do not ride the ocean surface. Instead, they move underwater, undetectable without the use of satellite imagery or sophisticated monitoring equipment. Despite their hidden nature, internal waves are fundamental parts of ocean water dynamics, transferring heat to the ocean depths and bringing up cold water from below. And they can reach staggering heights—some as tall as skyscrapers.

Because these waves are involved in ocean mixing and thus the transfer of heat, understanding them is crucial to global climate modeling, says Tom Peacock, a researcher at the Massachusetts Institute of Technology. Most models fail to take internal waves into account. "If we want to have more and more accurate climate models, we have to be able to capture processes such as this," Peacock says.

Peacock and his colleagues tried to do just that. Their study, published in November in *Geophysical Research Letters*, focused on internal waves generated in the Luzon Strait, which separates Taiwan and the Philippines. Internal waves in this region, thought to be some of the largest in the world, can reach about 500 meters high. "That's the same height as the Freedom Tower that's just been built in New York," Peacock says.

Although scientists knew of this phenomenon in the South China Sea and beyond, they didn't know exactly how internal waves formed. To find out, Peacock and a team of researchers from M.I.T. and Woods Hole Oceanographic Institution worked with France's National Center for Scientific Research using a giant facility there called the Coriolis Platform. The rotating platform, about 15 meters (49.2 feet) in diameter, turns at variable speeds and can simulate Earth's rotation. It also has walls, which means scientists can fill it with water and create accurate, large-scale simulations of various oceanographic scenarios.

Peacock and his team built a carbon-fiber resin scale model of the Luzon Strait, including the islands and surrounding ocean floor topography. Then they filled the platform with water of varying salinity to replicate the different densities found at the strait, with denser, saltier water below and lighter, less briny water above. Small particles were added to the solution and illuminated with lights from below in order to track how the liquid moved. Finally, they re-created tides using two large plungers to see how the internal waves themselves formed.

The Luzon Strait's underwater topography, with a distinct double-ridge shape, turns out to be responsible for generating the underwater waves. As the tide rises and falls and water moves through the strait, colder, denser water is pushed up over the ridges into warmer, less dense layers above it. This action results in bumps of colder water trailed by warmer water that generate an internal wave. As these waves move toward land, they become steeper—much the same way waves at the beach become taller before they hit the shore—until they break on a continental shelf.

The researchers were also able to devise a mathematical model that describes the movement and formation of these waves. Whereas the model is specific to the Luzon Strait, it can still help researchers understand how internal waves are generated in other places around the world. Eventually, this information will be incorporated into global climate models, making them more accurate. "It's very clear, within the context of these [global climate] models, that internal waves play a role in driving ocean circulations," Peacock says.

1. 文章来源

SAT 官方指南 Practice Test 3。

2. 文章分析

(1) 整篇文章话题——internal waves。

(2) 段落概要：P1：引出文章话题 internal waves，说明重要性；P2：科学家 Tom Peacock 认为了解 internal waves 非常重要；P3：Peacock 以 Luzon 海峡为案例进行研究；P4：了解 internal wave 的形成；P5：建立模型观测；P6：Luzon 海峡的 internal waves 具体形成过程；P7：继续建立数学模型。

文学类文章

文学类文章的阅读时间比科学类文章要长，因为处理的思路和方法不一样，而且基本上不能略读和跳读；特别是遇到充满对话的文学类文章，几乎要逐字逐句地阅读，而且还要理解语句背后的很多含义和态度。所以建议阅读时间在 5—6 分钟。在浏览文章时候重点标注：

1. 人物（characters）。
2. 人物关系（relationship）。
3. 人物性格特点（traits and personalities）。
4. 情感与态度（feelings and attitudes）。

人物是比较容易标注的，基本上遇到一个人名或是称谓就圈一下。这里需要注意的是同一个人物有不同的称谓，比如有篇官方试题中出现了 Edna 以及 Mrs. Pontellier，其实这是一个人。

其次要理解所有人物之间的关系，是父子关系、母女关系、朋友关系还是其他关系？这是需要在阅读时候理清楚的。

通常对于主要人物，一定会出现直接或是间接的性格描写。如果是通过形容词表达性格特点的，直接画线，如果是通过言行反映出来的，需要在旁边自行标注。

最后很重要的就是情感和态度。人物在某一时刻的内心情感是什么样的？他们之间的相互态度是正面还是负面的？这些问题也需要思考清楚。

下面通过一篇官方选取的文章进行示范。

This passage is adapted from P.G. Wodehouse, “Extricating Young Gussie.” Originally published in 1917.

She sprang it on me before breakfast. There in seven words you have a complete character sketch of my Aunt Agatha. I could go on indefinitely about brutality and lack of consideration. I merely say that she routed me out of bed to listen to her painful story somewhere in the small hours. It can’t have been half past eleven when Jeeves, my man, woke me out of the dreamless and broke the news:

‘Mrs Gregson to see you, sir.’

I thought she must be walking in her sleep, but I crawled out of bed and got into a dressing-gown. I knew Aunt Agatha well enough to know that, if she had come to see me, she was going to see me. That’s the sort of woman she is.

She was sitting bolt upright in a chair, staring into space. When I came in she looked at me in that darn critical way that always makes me feel as if I had gelatine where my spine ought to be. Aunt Agatha is one of those strong-minded women. I should think Queen Elizabeth must have been something like her. She bosses her husband, Spencer Gregson, a battered little chappie on the Stock Exchange. She bosses my cousin, Gussie Mannering-Phipps. She bosses her sister-in-law, Gussie’s mother. And, worst of all, she bosses me. She has an eye like a man-eating fish.

姑姑的性格特点描述，需要关注和总结

I dare say there are fellows in the world—men of blood and iron, don’t you know, and all that sort of thing—whom she couldn’t intimidate; but if you’re a chappie like me, fond of a quiet life, you simply curl into a ball when you see her coming, and hope for the best. My experience is that when Aunt Agatha wants you to do a thing you do it.

‘Hello, Aunt Agatha!’ I said.

‘Bertie,’ she said, ‘you look a sight. You look perfectly dissipated.’

I was feeling like a badly wrapped brown-paper parcel. I’m never at my best in the early morning. I said so.

‘Early morning! I had breakfast three hours ago, and have been walking in the park ever since, trying to compose my thoughts. I am extremely worried, Bertie. That is why I have come to you.’

And then I saw she was going to start something, and I bleated weakly to Jeeves to bring me tea. But she had begun before I could get it.

'What are your immediate plans, Bertie?'

'Well, I rather thought of tottering out for a bite of lunch later on, and then I might trickle off to Walton Heath for a round of golf.'

'I am not interested in your totterings and tricklings. I mean, have you any important engagements in the next week or so?'

I scented danger.

'Rather,' I said. 'Heaps! Millions! Booked solid!' 紧张而且害怕

'What are they?'

'I—er—well, I don't quite know.'

'I thought as much. You have no engagements. Very well, then, I want you to start immediately for America.'

'America!' 震惊的语气

Do not lose sight of the fact that all this was taking place on an empty stomach, shortly after the rising of the lark.

'Yes, America. I suppose even you have heard of America?' 'But why America?'

'Because that is where your Cousin Gussie is. He is in New York, and I can't get at him.'

'What's Gussie been doing?'

'Gussie is making a perfect idiot of himself.' 负面态度

To one who knew young Gussie as well as I did, the words opened up a wide field for speculation.

'In what way?'

'He has lost his head over a creature.' 指后文出现的女孩，表达了藐视

On past performances this rang true. Ever since he arrived at man's estate Gussie had been losing his head over creatures. He's that sort of chap. But, as the creatures never seemed to lose their heads over him, it had never amounted to much.

'I imagine you know perfectly well why Gussie went to America, Bertie. He is not clever, but he is very good-looking, and, though he has no title, the Mannering-Phippses are one of the best and oldest families in England. He had some excellent letters of introduction, and when he wrote home to say that he had met the most charming and beautiful girl in the world I felt quite happy. He continued to rave about her for several mails, and then this morning a letter has come from him in which he says, quite casually as a sort of afterthought, that he knows we are broadminded enough not to think any the worse of her because she is on the vaudeville stage.'

'Oh, I say!'

1. 人物

I (narrator)、Agatha、Gussie。

2. 人物关系

家庭关系，Agatha 是叙述者的姑姑，Gussie 是叙述者的堂兄弟。

3. 人物的性格特点

主要展现了姑姑的特点，为人有些专横跋扈。

4. 情感与态度

文章中很多对话展现了内省情感，参考文章备注。另外就是叙述者很害怕姑姑，他对堂兄弟的评价也是负面的，觉得他很愚蠢。

文学类文章读完之后，大家需要在脑海中展现出一个人物关系态度图。以这篇文章为例，大家需要呈现这样的画面：

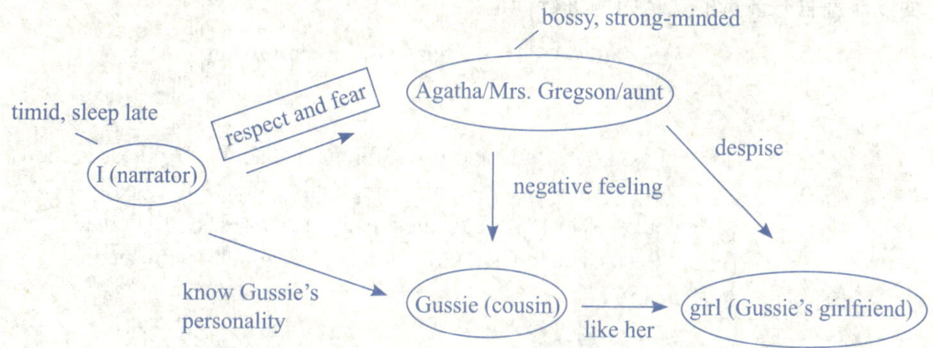

历史类文章

历史类文章通常节选自某位政治家的演讲、辩论、书信或是某本书的一部分，也可能来自某篇重要的政府文献。就目前真实考试的话题来看，大部分可以归为以下几种。

话题	官方试题举例
美国独立	2016 年 10 月亚太，Common Sense 节选
	2016 年 12 月亚太，Adams 书信评论独立
联邦邦联	2017 年 5 月亚太，有关弗吉尼亚制宪会议讨论联邦问题
	多篇可汗上历史类文章出现

女权运动	2016 年 5 月北美，Catharine Beecher 和 Angelina E. Grimké 文章节选
	2017 年 5 月北美，Mary Robinson 讨论女性教育问题
	官方指南 Test 1，Virginia Woolf, Three Guineas
	官方指南 Test 2，Elizabeth Cady Stanton’s address
	官方指南 Test 3，Talleyrand 和 Mary Wollstonecraft 讨论女权问题
政府法律	2016 年 5 月亚太，林肯和梭罗讨论人是否需要遵守法律
	2016 年 11 月亚太，法国大革命
	官方指南 Test 4，Edmund Burke 和 Thomas Paine 讨论有关个人与政府的关系
废奴运动	2017 年 1 月北美，林肯和道格拉斯辩论
工人运动	2016 年 3 月北美，罢工运动

历史类文章的阅读重点：

1. 确认文章话题。
2. 识别主要观点。
3. 寻找支撑原因。

下面以一篇官方节选的文章为例进行标记：

Questions 33–42 are based on the following passage.

Passage 1 is adapted from Abraham Lincoln, “Address to the Young Men’s Lyceum of Springfield, Illinois.” Originally delivered in 1838. Passage 2 is from Henry David Thoreau, “Resistance to Civil Government.” Originally published in 1849.

Passage 1

Let every American, every lover of liberty, every well wisher to his posterity, swear by the blood of the Revolution, never to violate in the least particular, the laws of the country; and never to tolerate their violation by others. As the patriots of seventy-six did to the support of the Declaration of Independence, so to the support of the Constitution and Laws, let every American pledge his life, his property, and his sacred honor;—let every man remember that to violate the law, is to trample on the blood of his father, and to tear the character of his own, and his children’s liberty. Let reverence for the laws, be breathed by every American mother, to the lisping babe, that prattles on her lap—let it be taught in schools, in

句首表达核心观点

后续用排比手法进行强调

seminaries, and in colleges;—let it be written in Primers, spelling books, and in Almanacs;—let it be preached from the pulpit, proclaimed in legislative halls, and enforced in courts of justice. And, in short, let it become the political religion of the nation; and let the old and the young, the rich and the poor, the grave and the gay, of all sexes and tongues, and colors and conditions, sacrifice unceasingly upon its altars...

防止别人误解自己的观点之后再强调观点——不应该违反法律

When I so pressingly urge a strict observance of all the laws, let me not be understood as saying there are no bad laws, nor that grievances may not arise, for the redress of which, no legal provisions have been made. I mean to say no such thing. But I do mean to say, that, although bad laws, if they exist, should be repealed as soon as possible, still while they continue in force, for the sake of example, they should be religiously observed. So also in unprovided cases. If such arise, let proper legal provisions be made for them with the least possible delay; but, till then, let them if not too intolerable, be borne with.

任何情况下暴民法都是不合适的

There is no grievance that is a fit object of redress by mob law. In any case that arises, as for instance, the promulgation of abolitionism, one of two positions is necessarily true; that is, the thing is right within itself, and therefore deserves the protection of all law and all good citizens; or, it is wrong, and therefore proper to be prohibited by legal enactments; and in neither case, is the interposition of mob law, either necessary, justifiable, or excusable.

Passage 2

先进行设问，然后用排比的反问表达观点

Unjust laws exist; shall we be content to obey them, or shall we endeavor to amend them, and obey them until we have succeeded, or shall we transgress them at once? Men generally, under such a government as this, think that they ought to wait until they have persuaded the majority to alter them. They think that, if they should resist, the remedy would be worse than the evil. But it is the fault of the government itself that the remedy is worse than the evil. It makes it worse. Why is it not more apt to anticipate and provide for reform? Why does it not cherish its wise minority? Why does it cry and resist before it is hurt? ...

If the injustice is part of the necessary friction of the machine of government, let it go, let it go;

分三种情况进行阐述如何应对不公正法律

perchance it will wear smooth—certainly the machine will wear out. If the injustice has a spring, or a pulley, or a rope, or a crank, exclusively for itself, then perhaps you may consider whether the remedy will not be worse than the evil; but if it is of such a nature that it requires you to be the agent of injustice to another, then, I say, break the law. Let your life be a counter friction to stop the machine. What I have to do is to see, at any rate, that I do not lend myself to the wrong which I condemn.

As for adopting the ways which the State has provided for remedying the evil, I know not of such ways. They take too much time, and a man's life will be gone. I have other affairs to attend to. I came into this world, not chiefly to make this a good place to live in, but to live in it, be it good or bad. A man has not everything to do, but something; and because he cannot do everything, it is not necessary that he should do something wrong...

文章选自 College Board The SAT Practice Test 6

主旨、结构题

主旨题主要考查对文章主旨的把握，题干通常以这样的形式出现：

- The author's central claim in the passage is that...
- The main/primary purpose of the passage is that...
- The main idea of the passage is that...

回答科学类和历史类文章的主旨题时，需要思考两大问题：

(1) 文章讨论什么？即话题 (topic)。

(2) 作者的观点和态度是什么？

另外，在判断选项的时候，如果上面两点都符合，那么需要判断哪个选项更全面。

而对于文学类文章的主旨题，主要是思考文章中的主要人物和情感 / 态度，也就是需要思考：

(1) 文章中的主要人物是哪些？

(2) 这些主要人物各自的性格特点是什么，相互的态度是什么？

(3) 有什么主要情节或者冲突？

结构题主要考查文章的行文思路，即先讲什么再讲什么。题干通常以这样的形式出现：

- Over the course of the passage, the main focus shifts from…

将题干和选项放在一起理解其实就是 main focus shifts from...to...，其中有这么几个关键词：

(1) focus（重点，焦点）也就是说，这类题型本质上还是考查对文章的概括。

(2) from...to...，也就是说，需要思考文章前部分和后部分的不同重点。

此外，需要注意 from...to... 对文章的划分不一定就是按照平均原则，可能是把文章第一段作为一个部分进行概括，然后把其余段落作为一个部分进行概括；也可能是把文章前面多个段落进行概括，然后对其余部分进行概括。

做这类题目时候，对于选项需要采取各个击破的原则。因为选项是通过 from...to... 呈现的，所以我们可以先判断 from 后面的内容是否正确，如果不正确也不用考虑 to 后面的内容了。只有两部分都正确的选项才是正确的。

本章例题

一、科学类文章

例 1

Questions 1–11 are based on the following passage.

This passage is excerpted from Luis Villareal, “Are Viruses Alive?” ©2008 by *Scientific American*. The symbol [2004] indicates that the following sentence is referenced in a question.

For about 100 years, the scientific community has repeatedly changed its collective mind over what viruses are. First seen as poisons, then as life-forms, then biological chemicals, viruses today are thought of as being in a gray area between living and nonliving: they cannot replicate on their own but can do so in truly living cells and can also affect the behavior of their hosts profoundly.

The seemingly simple question of whether or not viruses are alive has probably defied a simple answer all these years because it raises a fundamental issue: What exactly defines—life?A precise scientific definition of life is an elusive thing, but most observers would agree that life includes certain qualities in addition to an ability to replicate. For example, a living entity is in a state bounded by birth and death. Living organisms also are thought to require a degree of biochemical autonomy, carrying on the metabolic activities that produce the molecules and energy needed to sustain the organism. This level of autonomy is essential to most definitions.

Viruses, however, parasitize essentially all biomolecular aspects of life. That is, they depend on the host cell for the raw materials and energy necessary for nucleic acid synthesis, protein synthesis, processing and transport, and all other biochemical activities that allow the virus to multiply and spread. One might then conclude that even though these processes come under viral direction, viruses are simply non-living parasites of living metabolic systems. But a spectrum may exist between what is certainly alive and what is not.

A rock is not alive. A metabolically active sack, devoid of genetic material and the potential for propagation, is also not alive. A bacterium, though, is alive. Although it is a single cell, it can generate energy and the molecules needed to sustain itself, and it can reproduce. But what about a seed? A seed might not be considered alive. Yet it has a potential for life, and it may be destroyed. In this regard, viruses resemble seeds more than they do live cells.

Another way to think about life is as an emergent property of a collection of certain non-living things. Both life and consciousness are examples of emergent complex systems. They each require a critical level of complexity or interaction to achieve their respective states. A neuron by itself, or even in a network of nerves, is not conscious—whole brain complexity is needed. A virus, too, fails to reach a critical complexity. So life itself is an emergent, complex state, but it is made from the same fundamental, physical building blocks that constitute a virus. Approached from this perspective, viruses, though not fully alive, may be thought of as being more than inert matter: they verge on life.

In fact, in October [2004], French researchers announced findings that illustrate afresh just how close some viruses might come. Didier Raoult and his colleagues at the University of the Mediterranean in Marseille announced that they had sequenced the genome of the largest known virus, Mimivirus, which was discovered in 1992. The virus, about the same size as a small bacterium, infects amoebae. Sequence analysis of the virus revealed numerous genes previously thought to exist only in cellular organisms. Some of these genes are involved in making the proteins encoded by the viral DNA and may make it easier for Mimivirus to co-opt host cell replication systems. As the research team noted in its report in the journal *Science*, the enormous complexity of the Mimivirus's genetic complement "challenges the established frontier between viruses and parasitic cellular organisms."

【Question】

The main purpose of the passage is to

A) promote the work done by a team of researchers.

B) correct a common misunderstanding.

C) argue for an unpopular position.

D) explore reasons why a definition is ambiguous

【解析】文章在第一段即引出话题：what viruses are，之后主要讨论 viruses 到底是不是有生命的。所以这道题目只要确定了话题就能选出答案。

A 选项错误，因为 A 选项的话题是 work done a team of researchers，而文章目的并不是讲任何小组的研究工作。

B 选项错误，文章没有出现 misunderstanding，也无须纠正。

C 选项错误，文章并非支持某个不流行的观点。

D 正确，文章讨论对 viruses 的定义和认知，而且认为 viruses 在某种意义上是生命，但是又不是完全有生命。

例 2

Questions 1–11 are based on the following passage.

Adapted from Nani Morgan, Michael R. Irwin, Mei Chung, and Chenchen Wang, "The Effects of Mind-Body Therapies on the Immune System." © 2014 by Nani Morgan et al.

Over the last two decades, mind-body therapies (MBTs), including Tai Chi, Qi Gong, meditation, and Yoga have received increasing awareness and attention from the scientific community seeking to understand the safety and efficacy of these widely used practices. According to the 2007 National Health Interview Survey, 19% of American adults have used at least one mind-body therapy in the past 12 months. Currently, the National Center for Complementary and Alternative Medicine designates MBTs as a top research priority.

Previous work has shown that MBTs offer many

psychological and health functioning benefits including reductions in disease symptoms, improvements in coping, behavior regulation, quality of life, and well-being. In light of these benefits, recent investigations have sought to better understand the role of MBTs on physiological pathways such as the immune system. It has been well-established that psychological stress and depression impair anti-viral immune responses and activate innate immunity or markers of inflammation via effector pathways, such as the sympathetic nervous system and the hypothalamus-pituitary-adrenal (HPA) axis. In fact, behavioral interventions targeted at alleviating stress, promoting heightened states of relaxation, and encouraging moderate physical activity, have been shown to bolster anti-viral immune responses and decrease markers of inflammation, particularly among older adults or adults experiencing high levels of psychological stress.

The efficacy of such behavioral interventions in modulating the immune system suggests that MBTs may also confer immunomodulatory benefits. Tai Chi, Qi Gong, and Yoga are multi-dimensional behavioral therapies that integrate moderate physical activity, deep breathing, and meditation to promote stress reduction and relaxation, which could potentially influence the immune system. Meditation, including more integrative, mindfulness-based stress reduction programs, has also been shown to regulate emotional and affective responses to stress, and therefore may influence the immune system even in the absence of physical activity.

To our knowledge, this study is the first comprehensive review of the best available evidence, summarizing the effects of MBTs on the immune system while focusing on two aspects of immunity that are regulated by stress response mechanisms, namely inflammation and anti-viral related immune responses …Indeed, evidence accrued from 34 randomly controlled trials (RCTs) indicates that Tai Chi, Qi Gong, meditation, and Yoga, both short- and long-term, appear to reduce markers of inflammation and influence virus-specific immune responses to vaccinations. Our findings are supported by existing literature evaluating the immunomodulatory effects of other types of behavioral interventions including exercise, stress reduction, and mood modifying approaches. For example, exercise, one of the most widely-studied behavioral interventions, has been shown to reduce chronic inflammation, enhance immunological memory in the context of vaccination, and even reduce sick days associated with the common cold and other upper respiratory tract infections.

Apparently, powerful links exist between the brain and the immune system, and psychosocial factors can directly influence health through behavior. MBTs may buffer these immune alterations through relaxation, stress reduction, improved mood, and moderate physical activity. Behavioral responses are therefore the key to activating neuroendocrine and autonomic pathways, which in turn modulate the immune system and have implications for susceptibility to a variety of diseases. Thus, behavioral interventions that alter immune responses provide potent evidence for psychological influences on immune function.

【Question】

The main purpose of the passage is to

A) counter the claim that mind-body therapies have no effect on the immune system.

B) inform readers that mind-body therapies can influence immune responses in the body.

C) advance the argument that mind-body therapies have become an increasingly popular alternative.

D) uphold the findings of a previous study about the effect of mind-body therapies on behavior.

【解析】文章主要讨论 mind-body therapies，所以从话题来看四个选项都是正确的。其次，文章的主要观点是 mind-body therapies 对人的健康非常有益。所以从观点来看，答案应为 B（mind-body therapies can influence immune responses in the body）。

A 选项错误，因为文章并未出现这种需要反对的观点。

C 错误，因为观点不对；C 讲的是 mind-body therapies 变得越来越流行。

D 错误，因为观点不对；D 讲的是 mind-body therapies 影响行为，而文章讲的是对健康的益处。

例 3

Questions 1–11 are based on the following passage.

This passage is excerpted from Hiroshi Nittono, Michiko Fukushima, Akihiro Yano, and Hiroki Moriya, "The Power of Kawaii: Viewing Cute Images Promotes a Careful Behavior and Narrows Attentional Focus," © 2012 by Hiroshi Nittono, et al.

Line

Cute things are popular worldwide. In particular, Japan's culture accepts and appreciates childishness at the social level. Various kinds of anime and character goods, such as Pokémon and Hello Kitty, which are often described as kawaii, are produced and exported to many countries. This phenomenon attracts considerable attention from various fields, including aesthetics and engineering. Kawaii is an attributive adjective in modern Japanese and is often translated into English as "cute." However, this word was originally an affective adjective derived from an ancient word, kawa-hayu-shi, which literally means face (kawa)-flushing (hayu-shi). The original meaning of "ashamed, can't bear to see, feel pity" was changed to "can't leave someone alone, care for." In the present paper, we call this affective feeling, typically elicited by babies, infants, and young animals, cute.

Cute objects are assumed to be characterized by baby schema. This is a set of features that are commonly seen in young animals: a large head relative to the body size, a high and protruding forehead, large eyes, and so forth. Lorenz assumed that responses to baby schema are innate processes and are triggered by elemental features of the stimuli. In humans, the stimuli are deemed cute, capture attention, bring a smile to the viewer's face, and induce motivation and behavior for approach and caregiving. Baby schema modulates perception and attention at early stages of visual processing and activates the reward system of the brain. From an ethological perspective, it is understandable that cute things are treated favorably. However, little is known about whether encountering a cute object influences the subsequent behavior of the beholder. Because cute things produce positive feelings, their influence may extend to other aspects of behavior.

Sherman, Haidt, and Coan reported two experiments showing that performance in a fine motor dexterity task (the children's game Operation) improved after participants viewed a slide show of cute images (e.g., puppies and kittens) more than after they viewed images that were not as cute (e.g., dogs and cats). The performance measure was the number of plastic body parts that participants removed successfully from the body of the patient depicted on the game board using tweezers without touching the edges of the compartments. The improvement in the accuracy of this task can be interpreted as an index of increased attention to and control of motor actions. Sherman et al. explained this effect in terms of the embodied cognition perspective. That is, the tenderness elicited by cute images is more than just a positive affective feeling state. It can make people more physically tender in their motor behavior.

Although the results are intriguing, the mechanism of performance improvement remains unclear for two reasons. First, the time to complete the task was not measured. Better performance could be achieved either through slow and deliberate actions or through quick and accurate actions. Measuring the performance speed would help to explain the underlying mechanism. Second, only one type of task was used. If viewing baby animals induced a behavioral tendency toward protection and caregiving, performance improvement could be specific to a care-related task. The operation task used by Sherman et al. suggests caregiving because the player is expected to act as a doctor who helps the patient depicted on the game board with removing foreign objects from the patient's body. Using different types of tasks would elucidate the cause of performance improvement.

Recently, Sherman and Haidt challenged the classic view that cuteness is an innate releaser of parental instincts and caregiving responses. Instead, they proposed that perceiving cuteness motivates social engagement and primes affiliative, friendly tendencies. This attitudinal change is assumed to be linked with cognitive processes related to mentalizing (i.e., attributing mental states to agents) and sometimes indirectly leads to increased cares. If cuteness-induced behavioral carefulness is caused by a heightened motivation for social interaction, the effect would not be found in simple perceptual–cognitive tasks that do not suggest social interaction.

【Question】

The authors' central claim is that

A) cuteness provokes the same emotional responsesaround the world.

B) encountering a cute object may lead to changes inbehavior.

C) studies of cuteness should include tasks thatinvolve social interaction.

D) cuteness elicits feelings of tenderness in testsubjects.

【解析】这篇文章话题是 cute things，观点是 cute things 会正面地影响人的行为。所以答案是 B。

This passage is adapted from Steven C. Pan, "The Interleaving Effect: Mixing It Up Boosts Learning." © 2015 by *Scientific American*.

We've all heard the adage: practice makes perfect! In other words, acquiring skills takes time and effort. But how exactly does one go about learning a complex subject such as tennis, calculus, or how to play the violin? An age-old answer is: practice one skill at a time. A beginning pianist might rehearse scales before chords. A tennis player practices the forehand before the backhand. Learning researchers call this "blocking, " and because it is commonsensical and easy to schedule, blocking is dominant in schools and training programs, and other settings.

However, another strategy promises improved results. Enter "interleaving," a largely unheard-of technique that is capturing the attention of cognitive psychologists and neuroscientists. Whereas blocking involves practicing one skill at a time before the next (for example, "skill A" before —skill B and so on, forming the pattern "AAABBBCCC"), in interleaving one mixes, or interleaves, practice on several related skills together (forming for example the pattern "ABCABCABC"). For instance, a pianist alternates practice between scales, chords, and arpeggios, while a tennis player alternates practice between forehands, backhands, and volleys.

Given interleaving's promise, it is surprising then that few studies have investigated its utility in everyday applications. However, a new study by cognitive psychologist Doug Rohrer takes a step towards addressing that gap. Rohrer and his team are the first to implement interleaving in actual classrooms. The location: middle schools in Tampa, Florida. The target skills: algebra and geometry.

The three-month study involved teaching 7th graders slope and graph problems. Weekly lessons were largely unchanged from standard practice. Weekly homework worksheets, however, featured an interleaved or blocked design. When interleaved, both old and new problems of different types were mixed together. Of the nine participating classes, five used interleaving for slope problems and blocking for graph problems; the reverse occurred in the remaining four. Five days after the last lesson, each class held a review session for all students. A surprise final test occurred one day or one month later. The result? When the test was one day later, scores were 25 percent better for problems trained with interleaving; at one month later, the interleaving advantage grew to 76 percent.

These results are important for a host of reasons. First, they show that interleaving works in real-world, extended use. It is highly effective with an almost ubiquitous subject, math. The interleaving effect is long-term and the advantage over blocking actually increases with the passage of time. The benefit even persists when blocked materials receive additional review. Overall, the interleaving effect can be strong, stable, and long-lasting.

Researchers are now working to understand why interleaving yields such impressive results. One prominent explanation is that it improves the brain's ability to tell apart concepts. With blocking, once you know what solution to use, the hard part is over. With interleaving, each practice attempt is different from the last, so rote responses don't work. Instead, your brain must continuously focus on searching for different solutions. That process can improve your ability to learn critical features of skills.

A second explanation is that interleaving strengthens

memory associations. With blocking, a single strategy, temporarily held in short-term memory, is sufficient. That's not the case with interleaving—the correct solution changes from one practice attempt to the next. As a result, your brain is continually engaged at retrieving different responses and bringing them into short-term memory.

Both of these accounts imply that increased effort during training is needed when interleaving is used. This corresponds to a potential drawback of the technique, namely that the learning process often feels more gradual and difficult at the outset. However, that added effort can generate better, longer-lasting results.

【Question】

Over the course of the passage, the main focus shifts from

A) an evaluation of a popular learning strategy to a consideration of several lesser-known but potentially more effective strategies.

B) a presentation of experts' opinions on two learning strategies to an argument based on the author's own opinion.

C) an explanation of two learning strategies to a discussion of a study that shows the benefits of one strategy over the other.

D) a description of the learning strategies traditionally used by musicians and athletes to a recommendation to employ an alternative strategy.

【解析】文章第一段引出话题—— practice，并且解释了一种常见的练习方法 blocking；第二段提出另外一种方法 interleaving；第三段引出一位学者的实验研究；第四段是实验的过程和结果——interleaving 这种练习方法更好；第五段讲解结果的重要性和原因；第六、七两段分析为什么 interleaving 更好；第八段是总结。

选项 A，an evaluation of a popular learning strategy 错误，因为开头是说 blocking，但是没有 evaluate；而且后面 a consideration of several lesser-known but potentially more effective strategies，没有 several，只有 interleaving 这一种方法。

选项 B，a presentation of experts' opinions on two learning strategies 错误，因为前面没有出现专家对两种方法的看法；当然后面更没有提出作者自己的观点。

选项 C，an explanation of two learning strategies 正确，因为文章 1—2 段提出了两种学习策略；a discussion of a study that shows the benefits of one strategy over the other 正确，后面主要通过一个实验证明了 interleaving 比 blocking 更好。所以 C 正确。

选项 D，a description of the learning strategies traditionally used by musicians and athletes 这个描述过于细节化，并非文章的 focus。

Questions 1–11 are based on the following passage.

This passage is excerpted from Yan Zhao, "Aspirin-Like Compound Primes Plant Defense Against Pathogens," © 2014 by Yan Zhao.

Willow trees are well-known sources of salicylic acid, and for thousands of years, humans have extracted the compound from the tree's bark to alleviate minor pain, fever, and inflammation.

Now, salicylic acid may also offer relief to crop plants by priming their defenses against a microbial menace known as "potato purple top phytoplasma. " Outbreaks of the cell-wall-less bacterium in the fertile Columbia Basin region of the Pacific Northwest in 2002 and subsequent years inflicted severe yield and quality losses on potato crop. The Agricultural Research Service identified an insect accomplice —the beet leafhopper, which transmits the phytoplasma to plants while feeding.

Carefully timed insecticide applications can deter such feeding. But once infected, a plant cannot be cured. Now, a promising lead has emerged. An ARS-University of Maryland team has found evidence that pretreating tomato plants, a relative of potato, with salicylic acid can prevent phytoplasma infections or at least diminish their severity. Treating crops with salicylic acid to help them fend off bacteria, fungi, and viruses isn't new, but there are no published studies demonstrating its potential in preventing diseases caused by phytoplasmas.

Wei Wu, a visiting scientist, investigated salicylic acid's effects, together with molecular biologist Yan Zhao and others at ARS's Molecular Plant Pathology Laboratory in

Beltsville, Maryland. —This work reached new frontiers by demonstrating that plants could be beneficially treated even before they become infected and by quantifying gene activity underlying salicylic acid's preventive role, according to Robert E. Davis, the lab's research leader.

For the study, published in the July 2012 Annals of Applied Biology, the team applied two salicylic acid treatments to potted tomato seedlings. The first application was via a spray solution 4 weeks after the seedlings were planted. The second was via a root drench 2 days before phytoplasma-infected scions were grafted onto the plants' stems to induce disease. A control group of plants was not treated.

In addition to visually inspecting the plants for disease symptoms, the team analyzed leaf samples for the phytoplasma's unique DNA fingerprint, which turned up in 94 percent of samples from untreated plants but in only 47 percent of treated ones. Moreover, symptoms in the treated group were far milder than in untreated plants. In fact, analysis of mildly infected treated plants revealed phytoplasma levels 300 times below those of untreated plants, meaning that the salicylic acid treatment must have suppressed pathogen multiplication. Significantly, the remaining 53 percent of treated plants were symptom-and pathogen-free 40 days after exposure to the infected scions.

Researchers credit salicylic acid with triggering "systemic acquired resistance," a state of general readiness against microbial or insect attack. Using quantitative polymerase chain reaction procedures, the team also identified three regulatory defense genes whose activity was higher in treated plants than in untreated ones.

Why salicylic acid had this effect isn't known. Other questions remain as well, including how treated plants will fare under field conditions. Nonetheless, such investigations could set the stage for providing growers of potato, tomato, and other susceptible crops some insurance against phytoplasmas in outbreak-prone regions.

【Question】

Over the course of the passage, the main focus shifts from

A) an overview of all research done to date on a scientific topic to the future opportunities for studying this topic.

B) background information needed to understand an experiment to a description of the experiment itself.

C) a summary of the experiments leading to a particular scientific discovery to a philosophical discussion of the discovery's implications.

D) a description of a scientific inquiry to a description of the pivotal moments in solving a mystery related to that inquiry

【解析】文章第一段引出话题——salicylic acid。第二段说水杨酸也可以为植物提供治疗。第三段到最后是通过一个实验来证明水杨酸在防治疾病中的效果。

选项 A，an overview of all research done to date on a scientific topic 错误，文章前面没有对所有研究的概括。

选项 B，background information needed to understand an experiment 正确，对应第一段和第二段，属于实验的背景信息；a description of the experiment itself 正确，后面段落都是描述这个实验。所以正确答案是 B。

选项 C，a summary of the experiments leading to a particular scientific discovery 错误。前面并非对实验的总结。

选项 D，a description of a scientific inquiry 可以算作正确；a description of the pivotal moments in solving a mystery related to that inquiry 错误，文章后面没有描述实验中的重大时刻。

二、文学类文章

Questions 1–11 are based on the following passage.

This passage is excerpted from Edith Wharton, *The House of Mirth*, originally published in 1905.

Selden paused in surprise. In the afternoon rush of the Grand Central Station his eyes had been refreshed by the sight of Miss Lily Bart.

It was a Monday in early September, and he was returning to his work from a hurried dip into the country; but what was Miss Bart doing in town at that season? Her desultory air perplexed him. She stood apart from the crowd, letting it drift by her to the platform or the street, and wearing an air of irresolution which might, as he surmised, be the mask of a very definite purpose. It struck him at once that she was waiting for someone, but he hardly knew why the idea arrested him. There was nothing new about Lily Bart, yet he could never see her without a faint movement of interest: it was characteristic of her that she always roused speculation, that her simplest acts seemed the result of far-reaching intentions.

An impulse of curiosity made him turn out of his direct line to the door, and stroll past her. He knew that if she did not wish to be seen she would contrive to elude him; and it amused him to think of putting her skill to the test. "Mr. Selden—what good luck!"

She came forward smiling, eager almost, in her resolve to intercept him. One or two persons, in brushing past them, lingered to look; for Miss Bart was a figure to arrest even the suburban traveller rushing to his last train.

Selden had never seen her more radiant. Her vivid head, relieved against the dull tints of the crowd, made her more conspicuous than in a ball-room, and under her dark hat and veil she regained the girlish smoothness, the purity of tint, that she was beginning to lose after eleven years of late hours and indefatigable dancing.

"What luck!" she repeated. "How nice of you to come to my rescue!"

He responded joyfully that to do so was his mission in life, and asked what form the rescue was to take.

"Oh, almost any—even to sitting on a bench and talking to me. One sits out a cotillion—why not sit out a train? It isn't a bit hotter here than in Mrs. Van Osburgh's conservatory—and some of the women are not a bit uglier." She broke off, laughing, to explain that she had come up to town from Tuxedo, on her way to the Gus Trenors' at Bellomont, and had missed the three-fifteen train to Rhinebeck. "And there isn't another till half-past five." She consulted the little jewelled watch among her laces. "Just two hours to wait. And I don't know what to do with myself. My maid came up this morning to do some shopping for me, and was to go on to Bellomont at one o'clock, and my aunt's house is closed, and I don't know a soul in town." She glanced plaintively about the station. "It IS hotter than Mrs. Van Osburgh's, after all. If you can spare the time, do take me somewhere for a breath of air."

He declared himself entirely at her disposal: the adventure struck him as diverting. As a spectator, he had always enjoyed Lily Bart; and his course lay so far out of her orbit that it amused him to be drawn for a moment into the sudden intimacy which her proposal implied.

"Shall we go over to Sherry's for a cup of tea?"

She smiled assentingly, and then made a slight grimace.

"So many people come up to town on a Monday—one is sure to meet a lot of bores. I'm as old as the hills, of course, and it ought not to make any difference; but if I'm old enough, you're not," she objected gaily. "I'm dying for tea—but isn't there a quieter place?"

He answered her smile, which rested on him vividly. Her discretions interested him almost as much as her imprudences: he was so sure that both were part of the same carefully-elaborated plan. In judging Miss Bart, he had always made use of the "argument from design."

【Question】

Which choice best summarizes the passage?

A) The passage presents a portrait of two characters who decide to travel together

B) The passage explains the reasons for one character's avoidance of a community

C) The passage captures one character's fascination with another character

D) The passage describes a busy train station and the characters who inhabit it

【解析】文章中的两个主要人物，Selden 和 Miss Lily Bart。从文章可以看出来，Selden 是比较爱慕那位女生的，而后面主要是他们在车站的对话。答案选 C。

A 错误，因为并未提到他们决定一起旅行。

B 错误，因为并未提到其中一个人物在逃避社会。

D 错误，因为文章重点不是描写车站。

例 2

Questions 1–10 are based on the following passage.

This passage is excerpted from Jules Verne, *Around the World in Eighty Days*. Originally published in 1873.

The mansion in Saville Row, though not sumptuous, was exceedingly comfortable. The habits of its occupant were such as to demand but little from the sole domestic, but Phileas Fogg required him to be almost superhumanly prompt and regular. On this very 2nd of October he had dismissed James Forster, because that luckless youth had brought him shaving-water at eighty-four degrees Fahrenheit instead of eighty-six; and he was awaiting his successor, who was due at the house between eleven and half-past.

Phileas Fogg was seated squarely in his armchair, his feet close together like those of a grenadier on parade, his hands resting on his knees, his body straight, his head erect; he was steadily watching a complicated clock which indicated the hours, the minutes, the seconds, the days, the months, and the years. At exactly half-past eleven Mr. Fogg would, according to his daily habit, quit Saville Row, and repair to the Reform.[1] A rap at this moment sounded on the door of the cosy apartment where Phileas Fogg was seated, and James Forster, the dismissed servant, appeared.

"The new servant," said he.

A young man of thirty advanced and bowed.

"You are a Frenchman, I believe," asked Phileas Fogg, "and your name is John?"

"Jean, if monsieur pleases," replied the newcomer, "Jean Passepartout, a surname which has clung to me because I have a natural aptness for going out of one business into another. I believe I'm honest, monsieur, but, to be outspoken, I've had several trades. I've been an itinerant singer, a circus-rider, when I used to vault like Leotard,[2] and dance on a rope like Blondin.[3] Then I got to be a professor of gymnastics, so as to make better use of my talents; and then I was a sergeant fireman at Paris, and assisted at many a big fire. But I quitted France five years ago, and, wishing to taste the sweets of domestic life, took service as a valet here in England. Finding myself out of place, and hearing that Monsieur Phileas Fogg was the most exact and settled gentleman in the United Kingdom, I have come to monsieur in the hope of living with him a tranquil life, and forgetting even the name of Passepartout."

"Passepartout suits me," responded Mr. Fogg. "You are well recommended to me; I hear a good report of you. You know my conditions?"

"Yes, monsieur."

"Good! What time is it?"

"Twenty-two minutes after eleven," returned Passepartout, drawing an enormous silver watch from the depths of his pocket.

"You are too slow," said Mr. Fogg.

"Pardon me, monsieur, it is impossible—"

"You are four minutes too slow. No matter; it's enough to mention the error. Now from this moment, twenty-nine minutes after eleven, a.m., this Wednesday, 2nd October, you are in my service."

Phileas Fogg got up, took his hat in his left hand, put it on his head with an automatic motion, and went off without a word.

Passepartout heard the street door shut once; it was his new master going out. He heard it shut again; it was his predecessor, James Forster, departing in his turn. Passepartout remained alone in the house in Saville Row

[1]A Private members' club in London

[2]A French acrobat

[3]A French tightrope walker and acrobat

【Question】

Over the course of the passage, the main focus shifts from

A) a description of one character to an illustration of that character's interactions with another character.

B) a characterization of the upper classes to an exposure of problems with the social order.

C) a depiction of a particular place and time to a prediction about one man's future.

D) opinions held by an employer to the views asserted by a potential employee.

【解析】文章主要人物和人物关系为：Phileas Fogg（主人）、James Forster（被解雇的仆人）、Passepartout（新聘仆人）。通过阅读文章可以发现，主人的性格特点是生活非常规律，而且严苛要求仆人。

选项 A，a description of one character 正确，文章前面第一段和第二段主要介绍主人的特点；an illustration of that character's interactions with another character 正确，后文主要介绍主人和 James Forster 的对话（interactions）。所以答案选 A。

选项 B 错误，文章话题并非社会阶层，这个属于过度推测。

选项 C 错误，因为文章重点不是描写时间、地点或某人的未来。

选项 D 错误，因为文章重点并非老板和员工的观点。

例 3

Questions 1–11 are based on the following passage.

This passage is excerpted from Nathaniel Hawthorne, *The House of the Seven Gables*. Originally published in 1851. In this scene, set in the American Colonies when they were still governed by England, Colonel Pyncheon holds a party at his home for a visiting English dignitary.

One inauspicious circumstance there was, which awakened a hardly concealed displeasure in the breasts of a few of the more punctilious visitors. The founder of this stately mansion —a gentleman noted for the square and ponderous courtesy of his demeanor, ought surely to have stood in his own hall,and to have offered the first welcome to so many eminent personages as here presented themselves in honor of his solemn festival. He was as yet invisible; the most favored of the guests had not beheld him. This sluggishness on Colonel Pyncheon's part became still more unaccountable, when the second dignitary of the province made his appearance, and found no more ceremonious a reception. The lieutenant governor, although his visit was one of the anticipated glories of the day, had alighted from his horse, and assisted his lady from her side-saddle, and crossed the Colonel's threshold, without other greeting than that of the principal domestic.

This person—a gray-headed man, of quiet and most respectful deportment—found it necessary to explain that his master still remained in his study, or private apartment; on entering which, an hour before, he had expressed a wish on no account to be disturbed.

"Do not you see, fellow," said the high-sheriff of the county, taking the servant aside, "that this is no less a man than the lieutenant-governor? Summon Colonel Pyncheon at once! I know that he received letters from England this morning; and, in the perusal and consideration of them, an hour may have passed away without his noticing it. But he will be ill-pleased, I judge, if you suffer him to neglect the courtesy due to one of our chief rulers, and who may be said to represent King William, in the absence of the governor himself. Call your master instantly."

"Nay, please your worship," answered the man, in much perplexity, but with a backwardness that strikingly indicated the hard and severe character of Colonel Pyncheon's domestic rule; "my master's orders were exceeding strict; and, as your worship knows, he permits of no discretion in the obedience of those who owe him service. Let who list open yonder door; I dare not, though the governor's own voice should bid me do it!"

"Pooh, pooh, master high sheriff!" cried the lieutenant-governor, who had overheard the foregoing discussion, and felt himself high enough in station to play a little with his dignity. "I will take the matter into my own hands. It is time that the good Colonel came forth to greet his friends; else we shall be apt to suspect that he has taken a sip too much of his Canary wine, in his extreme deliberation which cask it were best to broach in honor of the day! But since he is so much behindhand, I will give him a remembrancer myself!"

Accordingly, with such a tramp of his ponderous riding-boots as might of itself have been audible in the remotest of the seven gables, he advanced to the door, which the servant pointed out, and made its new panels reecho with a loud, free knock. Then, looking round, with a smile, to the spectators, he awaited a response. As none came, however, he knocked again, but with the same unsatisfactory result as at first. And now, being a trifle choleric in his temperament, the lieutenant-governor uplifted the heavy hilt of his sword, wherewith he so beat and banged upon the door, that, as some of the bystanders whispered, the racket might have disturbed the dead. Be that as it might, it seemed to produce no awakening effect on Colonel Pyncheon. When the sound subsided, the silence through the house was deep, dreary, and oppressive, notwithstanding that the tongues of many of the guests had already been loosened by a surreptitious cup or two of wine or spirits.

"Strange, forsooth!—very strange!" cried the lieutenant-governor, whose smile was changed to a frown. "But seeing that our host sets us the good example of forgetting ceremony, I shall likewise throw it aside, and make free to intrude on his privacy."

He tried the door, which yielded to his hand, and was flung wide open by a sudden gust of wind that passed, as with a loud sigh, from the outermost portal through all the passages and apartments of the new house. It rustled the silken garments of the ladies, and waved the long curls of the gentlemen's wigs, and shook the window-hangings and the curtains of the bedchambers; causing everywhere a singular stir, which yet was more like a hush. A shadow of awe and half-fearful anticipation—nobody knew wherefore, nor of what—had all at once fallen over the company.

【Question】

Over the course of the passage, the main focus shifts from

A) the unusual behavior of a single character to a general sense of mystery.

B) the characterization of the party guests to the actions of the host.

C) a celebration of a certain social class to the denunciation of that class.

D) a description of a bygone era to a lament for the passing of that era.

【解析】文章引言中给出了很多重要信息，一个主人办了 party 来迎接一个英国高官。第一段主要强调这个主人并没有出来迎接客人和高官；第三段出现了仆人与高官的对话；后面几段主要描写那个 governor 自己踹门并拿剑柄敲门，但是始终无果。最后一段说突然一阵风吹开了门，也吹起了男性的假发和女性的服饰。

所以这道题的答案为 A，unusual behavior of a single character 指的是主人的不出现非常奇怪，然后 a general sense of mystery 指的是最后一段的神秘情景。

三、历史类文章

例 1

Questions 1–11 are based on the following passage.

This passage is adapted from a letter written by Thomas Jefferson to James Madison. It was originally written in 1785, when Jefferson was residing in France.

Seven o'clock, and retired to my fireside, I have determined to enter into conversation with you. This is a village of about 5,000 inhabitants when the court is not here and 20,000 when they are, occupying a valley thro' which runs a brook, and on each side of it a ridge of small mountains most of which are naked rock. The king comes here in the fall always, to hunt. His court attend him, as do also the foreign diplomatic corps. But as this is not indispensably required, and my finances do not admit the expense of a continued residence here, I propose to come occasionally to attend the king's levees, returning again to Paris, distant 40 miles.

This being the first trip, I set out yesterday morning to take a view of the place. For this purpose I shaped my course towards the highest of the mountains in sight, to the top of which was about a league. As soon as I had got clear of the town I fell in with a poor woman walking at the same rate with myself and going the same course. Wishing to know the condition of the labouring poor I entered into conversation with her, which I began by enquiries for the path which would lead me into the mountain: and thence proceeded to enquiries into her vocation, condition and circumstance. She told me she was a day labourer, at 8. sous or 4 d. sterling the day; that she had two children to maintain, and to pay a rent of 30 livres for her house (which would consume the hire of 75 days), that often she could get no employment, and of course was without bread. As we had walked together near a mile and she had so far served me as a guide, I gave her, on parting 24 sous. She burst into tears of a gratitude which I could perceive was unfeigned, because she was unable to utter a word. She had probably never before received so great an aid.

This little attendrissement[1], with the solitude of my walk led me into a train of reflections on that unequal division of property which occasions the numberless instances of wretchedness which I had observed in this country and is to be observed all over Europe. The property of this country is absolutely concentered in a very few hands, having revenues of from half a million of guineas a year downwards. These employ the flower of the country as servants, some of them having as many as 200 domestics, not labouring. They employ also a great number of manufacturers, and tradesmen, and lastly the class of labouring husbandmen[2]. But after all these comes the most numerous of all the classes, that is, the poor who cannot find work. I asked myself what could be the reason that so many should be permitted to beg who are willing to work, in a country where there is a very considerable proportion of uncultivated lands? These lands are kept idle mostly for the sake of game. It should seem then that it must be because of the enormous wealth of the proprietors which places them above attention to the increase of their revenues by permitting these lands to be labored.

I am conscious that an equal division of property is impracticable. But the consequences of this enormous inequality producing so much misery to the bulk of mankind, legislators cannot invent too many devices for subdividing property, only taking care to let their subdivisions go hand in hand with the natural affections of the human mind. The descent of property of every kind therefore to all the children, or to all the brothers and sisters, or other relations in equal degree is a politic measure, and a practicable one. Another means of silently lessening the inequality of property is to exempt all from taxation below a certain point, and to tax the higher portions of property in geometrical progression as they rise. Whenever there is in any country, uncultivated lands and unemployed poor, it is clear that the laws of property have been unemployed poor, it is clear that the laws of property have been so far extended as to violate natural right. The earth is given as a common stock for man to labour and live on. If for the encouragement of industry we allow it to be appropriated, we must take care that other employment be furnished to those excluded from the appropriation...

[1]emotion
[2]farmers

【Question】

Jefferson's central claim in the passage is that

A) the current system of inheritance and ownership is unlikely ever to change.

B) wealth should be redistributed in a way that benefits the majority of society.

C) the unemployed should use their energies to work the land, rather than ask for money.

D) everybody has the natural right to as much property as he or she thinks necessary.

【解析】文章段落概要：第一段先介绍当时居住的环境和背景——法国的某个小镇；第二段说了一个故事，偶遇一位贫困妇女；第三段开始阐述自己的情感和思考，有关财富的分配不均；第四段给出一些解决方案。

所以整篇文章的话题是财富分配不均，之后提出解决方案。答案选 B。

A 错误，因为话题错误，并非讲继承和所有权。

C 错误，因为话题错误，并非讲失业者应该怎么办。

D 错误，因为观点错误，并非每个人都有获得自己认为必要的财产的权利。

例 2

Questions 1–11 are based on the following passage.

The following is a speech given by Benjamin Franklin to the Constitutional Convention on September 17, 1787. The Convention was deciding whether to ratify the final version of the U.S. Constitution.

Dear Mr. President,

I confess that there are several parts of this constitution which I do not at present approve, but I am not sure I shall never approve them: For having lived long, I have experienced many instances of being obliged by better information or fuller consideration, to change opinions even on important subjects, which I once thought right, but found to be otherwise. It is therefore that the older I grow, the more apt I am to doubt my own judgment, and to pay more respect to the judgment of others. Most men indeed as well as most sects in Religion, think themselves in possession of all truth, and that wherever others differ from them it is so far error. Steele, a Protestant in a Dedication tells the Pope, that the only difference between our Churches in their opinions of the certainty of their doctrines is, the Church of Rome is infallible and the Church of England is never in the wrong. But though many private persons think almost as highly of their own infallibility as of that of their sect, few express it so naturally as a certain French lady, who in a dispute with her sister, said "I don't know how it happens, Sister but I meet with no body but myself, that's always in the right..."

In these sentiments, Sir, I agree to this Constitution with all its faults, if they are such; because I think a general Government necessary for us, and there is no form of Government but what may be a blessing to the people if well administered, and believe farther that this is likely to be well administered for a course of years, and can only end in Despotism, as other forms have done before it, when the people shall become so corrupted as to need despotic Government, being incapable of any other. I doubt too whether any other Convention we can obtain may be able to make a better Constitution. For when you assemble a number of men to have the advantage of their joint wisdom, you inevitably assemble with those men, all their prejudices, their passions, their errors of opinion, their local interests, and their selfish views.

From such an Assembly can a perfect production be expected? It therefore astonishes me, Sir, to find this system approaching so near to perfection as it does; and I think it will astonish our enemies, who are waiting with confidence to hear that our councils are confounded like those of the Builders of Babel*; and that our States are on the point of separation, only to meet hereafter for the purpose of cutting one another's throats. Thus I consent, Sir, to this Constitution because I expect no better, and because I am not sure, that it is not the best. The opinions I have had of its errors, I sacrifice to the public good—I have never whispered a syllable of them abroad —Within these walls they were born, and here they shall die— If every one of us in returning to our Constituents were to report the objections he has had to it, and endeavor to gain partizans in support of them, we might prevent its being generally received, and thereby lose all the salutary effects & great advantages resulting naturally in our favor among foreign Nations as well as among ourselves, from our real or apparent unanimity. Much of the strength & efficiency of any Government in procuring and securing happiness to the people, depends on opinion, on the general opinion of the goodness of the Government, as well as of the wisdom and integrity of its Governors. I hope therefore that for our own sakes as a part of the people, and for the sake of posterity, we shall act heartily and unanimously in recommending this Constitution (if approved by Congress & confirmed by the Conventions) wherever our influence may extend, and turn our future thoughts & endeavors to the means of having it well administered.

On the whole, Sir, I cannot help expressing a wish that every member of the Convention who may still have objections to it, would with me, on this occasion doubt a little of his own infallibility—and to make manifest our unanimity,put his name to this instrument

*In the Christian Bible, the people who built the Tower of Babel spoke multiple languages and could not understand each other well enough to complete the tower's construction.

【Question】

The author's central claim in the passage is that

A) the Constitution will have to suffice until it is proven to be inadequate.

B) the objections to the Constitution are trivial and should be disregarded by the Assembly.

C) the objections to the Constitution can be dismissed unless they are unanimous.

D) the Constitution is adequate and should be passed without objection.

【解析】整篇文章通过第一段就可以得出话题和观点。文章开头其实是让步，首先承认宪法有些地方作者是不同意的，之后立即转折，不确定是否永远不赞同。这个转折表明作者其实是认同这部宪法的。第二段开头也直接表达了 agree to this Constitution with all its faults，第三段认为宪法能够这样已经很好了（虽然不完美），而且敌人希望他们意见不统一之后分裂。

所以，整篇文章讨论是否通过宪法，观点是支持通过宪法。答案选择 D。

A 选项错误，因为观点不对。

B 选项错误，因为文章的话题并非在说对宪法的反对是不重要的，而是通过宪法的必要性和原因。

C 选项错误，因为观点错误，并非表达除非这些反对是一致的，否则就应该被 dismissed。

Questions 1-11 are based on the following passage.

This passage is excerpted from William Graham Sumner, “The Absurd Effort to Make the World Over," originally published in 1894. Sumner was an outspoken economist and highly influential sociology professor at Yale University.

It will not probably be denied that the burden of proof is on those who affirm that our social condition is utterly diseased and in need of radical regeneration. My task at present, therefore, is entirely negative and critical: to examine the allegations of fact and the doctrines which are put forward to prove the correctness of the diagnosis and to warrant the use of the remedies proposed.

When anyone asserts that the class of skilled and unskilled manual laborers of the United States is worse off now in respect to diet, clothing, lodgings, furniture, fuel, and lights; in respect to the age at which they can marry; the number of children they can provide for; the start in life which they can give to their children, and their chances of accumulating capital, than they ever have been at any former time, he makes a reckless assertion for which no facts have been offered in proof. Upon an appeal to facts, the contrary of this assertion would be clearly established. It suffices, therefore, to challenge those who are responsible for the assertion to make it good.

Nine-tenths of the socialistic and semi-socialistic, and sentimental or ethical, suggestions by which we are overwhelmed come from failure to understand the phenomena of the industrial organization and its expansion. It controls us all because we are all in it. It creates the conditions of our existence, sets the limits of our social activity, regulates the bonds of our social relations, determines our conceptions of good and evil, suggests our life-philosophy, molds our inherited political institutions, and reforms the oldest and toughest customs, like marriage and property. I repeat that the turmoil of heterogeneous and antagonistic social whims and speculations in which we live is due to the failure to understand what the industrial organization is and its all-pervading control over human life, while the traditions of our school of philosophy lead us always to approach the industrial organization, not from the side of objective study, but from that of philosophical doctrine. Hence it is that we find that the method of measuring what we see happening by what are called ethical standards, and of proposing to attack the phenomena by methods thence deduced, is so popular.

The advance of a new country from the very simplest social coordination up to the highest organization is a most interesting and instructive chance to study the development of the organization. It has of course been attended all the way along by stricter subordination and higher discipline. All organization implies restriction of liberty. The gain of power is won by narrowing individual range. The methods of business in colonial days were loose and slack to an inconceivable degree. The movement of industry has been all the time toward promptitude, punctuality, and reliability. It has been attended all the way by lamentations about the good old times; about the decline of small industries; about the lost spirit of comradeship between employer and employee; about the narrowing of the interests of the workman; about his conversion into a machine or into a "ware," and about industrial war. These lamentations have all had reference to unquestionable phenomena attendant on advancing organization. In all occupations the same movement is discernible in the learned professions, in schools, in trade, commerce, and transportation. It is to go on faster than ever, now that the continent is filled up by the first superficial layer of population over its whole extent and the intensification of industry has begun. The great inventions both make the intension of the organization possible and make it inevitable, with all its consequences, whatever they may be. I must expect to be told here, according to the current fashions of thinking, that we ought to control the development of the organization. The first instinct of the modern man is to get a law passed to forbid or prevent what, in his wisdom, he disapproves.

Now the intensification of the social organization is what

gives us greater social power. It is to it that we owe our increased comfort and abundance. We are none of us ready to sacrifice this. On the contrary, we want more of it. We would not return to the colonial simplicity and the colonial exiguity if we could. If not, then we must pay the price. Our life is bounded on every side by conditions.

【Question 1】

The main purpose of the passage is to

A) delineate the course of industrial progress.

B) question the practicality of democratic ideals.

C) encourage support for individual liberties.

D) highlight the uselessness of social reform.

【Question 2】

Over the course of the passage, the main focus shifts from

A) an overview of industrial advancement to a clarification of the problem.

B) an acknowledgement of the problem with industrial advancement to the proposal of a solution.

C) an assembling of arguments against industrial advancement to a justification of its effects.

D) an explanation of industrial advancement to an admission of the drawbacks

【解析】Question 1 整篇文章分析：从开头第一句即可以推测出作者观点，“It will not probably be denied that the burden of proof is on those who affirm that our social condition is utterly diseased and in need of radical regeneration.” 认为我们社会状况是病态的并需要剧烈的变革，需要提供证据。言外之意就是你们这么认为，但是没有实际的证据。如果第一句看不懂也没有关系，因为第二句也立即表明作者观点：My task at present, therefore, is entirely negative and critical. 表明作者对我们社会状况是病态的并需要剧烈的变革这种观点持负面的和批判的态度。

第二段强调的是 he makes a reckless assertion for which no facts have been offered in proof，继续批判持有这种观点的人。

第三段说明这些人并没有真正理解工业的发展，所以认为工业发展导致社会的“疾病”。

第四段阐述社会发展的必然性和工业社会的优越性以及有必要对人进行必要的控制。

最后一段最为总结，再次说明正是社会结构的加强才给我们带来舒适和丰富。

所以本题从话题上是为了批判那些认为社会需要变革的人。答案选择 D。

A 选项错误，因为文章重点和目的不在描述工业进步的过程。

B 选项错误，因为话题错误，并非讨论民主。

C 选项错误，因为话题错误，并非讨论个人自由。

Question 2 选项分析：A 选项，an overview of industrial advancement 错误，文章前面主要是批判对方观点，并非概括地介绍工业进步。

B 选项，an acknowledgement of the problem with industrial advancement 错误，作者并没有承认工业进步带来的问题。

C 选项，an assembling of arguments against industrial advancement 正确，前面提出了反对工业进步的观点；a justification of its effects 这里主要先确定 its 指什么，因为选项前面说提出很多反对工业进步的观点，its 指的是 industrial advancement。那么 justification of its effects 就是 justification of the effects of industrial advancement, 正确，因为后文都是阐述工业进步的优越性。

D 选项，an explanation of industrial advancement 勉强可以认为正确，因为文章第三段和第四段确实在解释工业进步；an admission of the drawbacks 明显错误，因为后面没有承认工业进步的缺点。

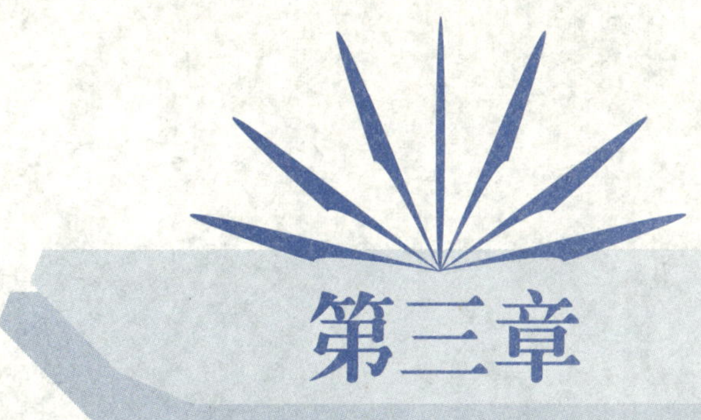

第三章

把握重点，什么才是重点？

在读句子和段落时候，其中一项非常重要的能力是区分重点和非重点。对于重点信息需要认真阅读，而非重点信息则可以一带而过。也就是说，读重点信息时需要放慢速度，而读非重点信息时则可以提速。

那么，如何区分重点和非重点信息呢？

在句子中，重点信息比较好寻找，就是找句子主干即可。比如：

And yet public transportation, in many minds, is the opposite of glamour—a squalid last resort for those with one too many impaired driving charges, too poor to afford insurance, or too decrepit to get behind the wheel of a car.

主干是：public transportation is the opposite of glamour. 仔细理解这句话即可把握整个句子的核心意思。

Looking forward, I think we will need to deploy different kinds of practices (especially new, mixed approaches that take the best of organic and conventional farming systems) where they are best suited—geographically, economically, socially, etc.

主干是：I think we will need to deploy different kinds of practices. 句子核心意思是需要采用不同的方法。

下面我们重点进行段落的重点和非重点信息区分，并通过这种区分来对段落进行概括。

段落的重要信息寻找

在段落中，我们需要通过判断句子的作用来区分重点和非重点信息。如果是抽象概括的句子那么就是重点信息；如果是具体细节的句子就是非重点信息。那么，实际段落中哪些是非重点信息呢？

1. 举例论证。
2. 有关一个理论/观点的具体解释。
3. 列举具体理由、研究或者数据以证明一个观点的正确。
4. 分类描述。
5. 排比论证。
6. 时间或者过程描述。

假设一个段落开头是重点信息，而后面都是细节，那么我们在阅读这个段落时的阅读速度是这样的。

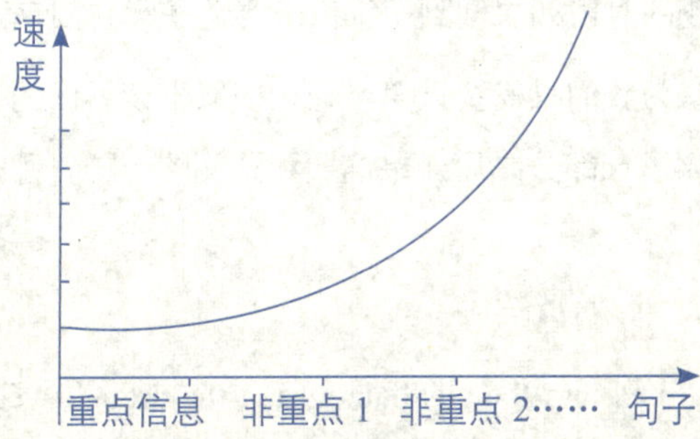

下面具体来说该如何阅读。

例 1

Ridiculing television, and warning about its inherent evils, is nothing new. It has been that way since the medium was invented, and television hasn't exactly been lavished with respect as the decades have passed. For the past several decades, television has been blamed for corrupting our youth and exciting our adults, distorting reality, and basically being a big, perhaps dangerous, waste of time. Before TV, radio and film were accused of the same things. And long before that—in fact, some 2,500 years earlier—philosophers were arguing that poetry and drama should be excluded from any ideal city on much the same grounds.

【解析】这个段落中，第一句话是概括性的句子：批判电视并不是新鲜事，言外之意就是很早就批判电视了。而后面从第二句开始讲解历史上如何批判电视，甚至在电视之前就批判收音机、电影以及诗歌、戏剧。虽然这个段落有 100 多个单词，但是在阅读的时候其实只需要关注如下所示的画线部分。

<u>Ridiculing television, and warning about its inherent evils, is nothing new. It has been that way since the medium was invented</u>, and television hasn't exactly been lavished with respect as the decades have passed. <u>For the past several decades, television has been blamed for</u> corrupting our youth and exciting our adults, distorting reality, and basically being a big, perhaps dangerous, waste of time. <u>Before TV, radio and film were accused</u> of the same things. <u>And long before that</u>—in fact, some 2,500 years earlier—philosophers were arguing that poetry and drama should be excluded from any ideal city on much the same grounds.

【解析】为什么可以这样去阅读？因为我们只要知道了第一句话的作用（批判电视不是新鲜事），就可以去预测（预测是非常重要的阅读方法）后面的内容可能是细节描写，比如从什么时候就开始批判、如何批判以及为什么批判。而读到第二句前半句就确定了这种预测；第三句还是以时间开头；第四句是更久远的时间……所以后面的内容不断在我们预测的方向上展开，由此阅读速度就可以迅速提升，而且不影响我们对段落的整体理解。

有些同学会说，我这样阅读很多细节没有看到啊。但是要知道我们在读第一遍的时候完全不用去记太多的细节，做题的时候如果问到了细节内容还是需要回来确认的。

另外，也不要错误地认为我们只需要读第一句！如果不读后面的内容如何知道它们不重要呢？但是后面的句子你在读了一部分之后如果确实和预测的一样，那么就不用仔细甚至逐字慢慢阅读了。

例 2

The first wells were drilled into the Ogallala during the drought years of the early 1930s. The ensuing rapid expansion of irrigation agriculture, especially from the 1950s onward, transformed the economy of the region. More than 100,000 wells now tap the Ogallala. Modern irrigation devices, each capable of spraying 4.5 million liters of water a day, have produced a landscape dominated by geometric patterns of circular green islands of crops. Ogallala water has enabled the High Plains region to supply significant amounts of the cotton, sorghum, wheat, and corn grown in the United States. In addition, 40 percent of American grain-fed beef cattle are fattened here.

【解析】这个段落开头第一句说的是一个事实：第一批水井是在 20 世纪 30 年代挖掘的。而第二句说灌溉农业的发展改变了当地的经济，这句话比较抽象，到底如何改变呢？所以可以预测后文应该全是举例。从第三句开始到最后，我们发现都是具体细节，比如灌溉设备产生了什么样的地貌，种植了什么农作物，甚至多少牛都是在那个地方喂养的。

那么，我们从第三句开始就可以提升自己的阅读速度了。

例 3

Let every American, every lover of liberty, every well wisher to his posterity, swear by the blood of the Revolution, never to violate in the least particular, the laws of the country; and never to tolerate their violation by others. As the patriots of seventy-six did to the support of *The Declaration of Independence*, so to the support of the Constitution and Laws, let every American pledge his life, his property, and his sacred honor; —let every man remember that to violate the law, is to trample on the blood of his father, and to tear the character of his own, and his children's liberty. Let reverence for the laws, be breathed by every American mother, to the lisping babe, that prattles on her lap—let it be taught in schools, in seminaries, and in colleges; —let it be written in Primers, spelling books, and in Almanacs; —let it be preached from the pulpit, proclaimed in legislative halls, and enforced in courts of justice. And, in short, let it become the political religion of the nation; and let the old and the young, the rich and the poor, the grave and the gay, of all sexes and tongues, and colors and conditions, sacrifice unceasingly upon its altars...

【解析】这个段落中，第一句就强烈呼吁：让每一个美国人、每一个热爱自由的人、每一个希望自己后代安康的人，永远不要违反任何国家法律，也不要容忍别人的违法。而后面每句话都是以 let 重复出现，运用了排比的手法。像这种排比的段落其实非常好处理，因为排比的句子一定具有同样的作用，因此只需要看懂第一句即可。所以，需要关注的词是如下画线的地方。

<u>Let every American, every lover of liberty, every well wisher to his posterity</u>, swear by the blood of the Revolution, <u>never to violate in the least particular, the laws of the country; and never to tolerate their violation by others</u>. As the patriots of seventy-six did to the support of the Declaration

of Independence, so to the support of the Constitution and Laws, let every American pledge his life, his property, and his sacred honor; —let every man remember that to violate the law, is to trample on the blood of his father, and to tear the character of his own, and his children's liberty. Let reverence for the laws, be breathed by every American mother, to the lisping babe, that prattles on her lap—let it be taught in schools, in seminaries, and in colleges; —let it be written in Primers, spelling books, and in Almanacs; —let it be preached from the pulpit, proclaimed in legislative halls, and enforced in courts of justice. And, in short, let it become the political religion of the nation; and let the old and the young, the rich and the poor, the grave and the gay, of all sexes and tongues, and colors and conditions, sacrifice unceasingly upon its altars...

例 4

Antipathy is the only word which can express the feeling Edward Crimsworth had for me—a feeling, in a great measure, involuntary, and which was liable to be excited by every, the most trifling movement, look, or word of mine. My southern accent annoyed him; the degree of education evinced in my language irritated him; my punctuality, industry, and accuracy, fixed his dislike, and gave it the high flavour and poignant relish of envy; he feared that I too should one day make a successful tradesman. Had I been in anything inferior to him, he would not have hated me so thoroughly, but I knew all that he knew, and, what was worse, he suspected that I kept the padlock of silence on mental wealth in which he was no sharer. If he could have once placed me in a ridiculous or mortifying position, he would have forgiven me much, but I was guarded by three faculties—Caution, Tact, Observation; and prowling and prying as was Edward's malignity, it could never baffle the lynx-eyes of these, my natural sentinels. Day by day did his malice watch my tact, hoping it would sleep, and prepared to steal snake-like on its slumber; but tact, if it be genuine, never sleeps.

【解析】这个段落第一句表明了 Edward Crimsworth 对我的态度——反感和厌恶；我的任何微不足道的行为、表情或是言语都会激起他的反感。所以我们合理地预测后文会进行细节描写——哪些行为、表情或者言语呢？从第二句开始提到我的口音和教育程度、我的守时和勤劳、我成功的可能性都让他厌恶和嫉妒。到最后用比喻和类比的修辞手法，再次强调 Edward Crimsworth 对我的敌意。所以阅读时候仍然可以采用“慢—预测—快”这种方式进行。

当然了，并不是所有段落最重要的句子都是第一句。如果段落中出现了转折或对比，那么这个地方更加重要，比如下面这个段落。

例 5

Most people know the gruesome story of Baron Victor Frankenstein, the arrogant doctor who created a living creature from the bodies of corpses, only to see his creation turn murderous. The story has been told and retold. It has also been the subject of numerous films, and most people are familiar with the tale, so much so that we use allusions, or references, to Frankenstein's monster to describe a good idea gone very wrong. What many people don't know, however, is that the chilling story of Dr. Frankenstein and his creature was written by a nineteen-year-old newlywed named Mary Shelley. As a young bride, Shelley liked to take part in storytelling competitions with her husband. On one particularly long evening in 1816, her husband Byron suggested that everyone compose a ghost story. In response to Byron's suggestion, Mary Shelley spent the night writing and was ready the next day with the story of Dr. Frankenstein, the man who constructed a creature from body parts and galvanized it into action. When she read it aloud, everyone agreed Shelley's story was the best by far, and by 1818 she had published it as a novel.

【解析】这个段落在第四句中出现了转折（信号词 however），那么这句话才是全段的核心。整个段落想突出这部小说的作者是当时只有 19 岁的 Mary Shelley。但是需要注意每段话开头第一句是一定要慢读的，因为是第一句。而从第二句开始需要判断是否重要信息，也就是判断第二句往后是第一句话的细节还是出现了转折；如果是细节，那么就可以读快，如果出现了转折，那么需要慢下来好好理解。

所以上面这个段落需要认真看的内容画线如下。

<u>Most people know the gruesome story of Baron Victor Frankenstein</u>, the arrogant doctor who created a living creature from the bodies of corpses, only to see his creation turn murderous. The story has been told and retold. <u>It has also been the subject of numerous films</u>, and most people are familiar with the tale, so much so that we use allusions, or references, to Frankenstein's monster to describe a good idea gone very wrong. <u>What many people don't know, however, is that the chilling story of Dr. Frankenstein and his creature was written by a nineteen-year-old newlywed named Mary Shelley</u>. As a young bride, <u>Shelley liked to take part in storytelling competitions</u> with her husband. On one particularly long evening in 1816, <u>her husband Byron suggested that everyone compose a ghost story</u>. In response to Byron's suggestion, <u>Mary Shelley spent the night writing</u> and was ready the next day with the story of Dr. Frankenstein, the man who constructed a creature from body parts and galvanized it into action. <u>When she read it aloud, everyone agreed Shelley's story was the best</u> by far, and by 1818 she had published it as a novel.

【解析】第一句处理主句即可，后面第二、三句仍然这样。第四句出现转折，所以需要更加仔细地阅读和理解；第四句往后大致是讲当时在什么情况下 Mary Shelley 创作出这部小说，属于细节描写，可以快读。对于这种段落，我们的阅读速度整体进程如下图。

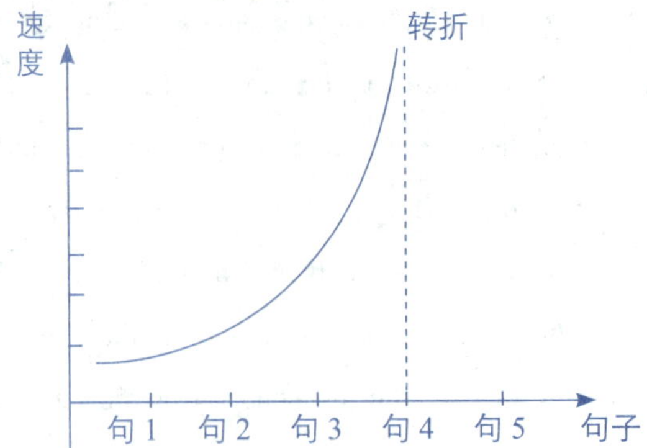

例 6

Reduction in numbers of game should have boded ill for their survival in later times. A worsening of the plight of deer was to be expected as settlers encroached on the land, logging, burning, and clearing, eventually replacing a wilderness landscape with roads, cities, towns, and factories. No doubt the numbers of deer declined still further. Recall the fate of the Columbian white-tailed deer, now in a protected status. But for the black-tailed deer, human pressure has had just the opposite effect. Wildlife zoologist Helmut Buechner (1953), in reviewing the nature of biotic changes in Washington through recorded time, says that "since the early 1940s, the state has had more deer than at any other time in its history, thewinter population fluctuating around approximately 320,000 deer (mule and black-tailed deer), which will yield about 65,000 of either sex and any age annually for an indefinite period."

【解析】这个段落在第五句 (But for the black-tailed deer…) 出现了转折；前面主要讲述人类活动对鹿 (比如 white-tailed deer) 的负面影响，而后面部分进行转折，提及对于 black-tailed deer，人类的活动对其影响恰恰相反。所以整个段落其实核心部分在中间的转折。再结合整个段落来看，是一个典型的对比结构段落。

那么，哪些信号词表示转折 / 对比的逻辑结构呢?

单词或短语： but、however、nonetheless、nevertheless、conversely、still、despite、unfortunately、yet、on the contrary、in contrast、now、20 years later...

句型： Things all changed when...

A surprising thing happened, ...

But it was not the case.

To the surprise of all, ...

……

通过重点信息对段落进行概括

在 SAT 题目中，有一种题型是专门考查学生对段落的概括。通常题干如下：

- What is the main purpose of paragraph?
- What function does the paragraph serve in the passage?
- The central idea of the paragraph is that...

这种题目本质上就是让考生知道段落的最重要信息是什么、最主要的目的和作用是什么。下面我们根据前面举的 6 个例子进行选项的挑选。

例 1

Ridiculing television, and warning about its inherent evils, is nothing new. It has been that way since the medium was invented, and television hasn't exactly been lavished with respect as the decades have passed. For the past several decades, television has been blamed for corrupting our youth and exciting our adults, distorting reality, and basically being a big, perhaps dangerous, waste of time. Before TV, radio and film were accused of the same things. And long before that—in fact, some 2,500 years earlier—philosophers were arguing that poetry and drama should be excluded from any ideal city on much the same grounds.

【Question】

What is the purpose of this paragraph?

A) criticize the way television distorts the truth

B) examine the evolution of television as a medium

C) place contemporary criticism of television in a historical context

D) directly compare television and drama as art forms

【解析】既然我们已经确定段落第一句为最重要的句子，所以这个段落就是说明批判电视其实由来已久。所以答案选择 C：在历史背景下来讨论对电视的批判。

例 2

The first wells were drilled into the Ogallala during the drought years of the early 1930s. The ensuing rapid expansion of irrigation agriculture, especially from the 1950s onward, transformed the economy of the region. More than 100,000 wells now tap the Ogallala. Modern irrigation devices, each capable of spraying 4.5 million liters of water a day, have produced a landscape dominated by geometric patterns of circular green islands of crops. Ogallala water has enabled the High Plains region to supply significant amounts of the cotton, sorghum, wheat, and corn grown in the United States. In addition, 40 percent of American grain-fed beef cattle are fattened here.

【Question】

What is the main idea of this paragraph?

A) It indicates that wells have a great influence on the economy in the region.

B) It shows that agriculture is an important component in that area.

C) It illustrates why beef cattle are fattened there.

D) It provides the number of wells drilled at a specific time.

【解析】通过理解重点句子，即可选出答案为 A。

B 选项错误，因为这个段落的主旨是水井，通过水井进行灌溉改变了当地经济，而不是说农业重要。

C 选项错误，因为这个是细节。

D 选项错误，因为这个是细节。

例 3

Let every American, every lover of liberty, every well wisher to his posterity, swear by the blood of the Revolution, never to violate in the least particular, the laws of the country; and never to tolerate their violation by others. As the patriots of seventy-six did to the support of the Declaration of Independence, so to the support of the Constitution and Laws, let every American pledge his life, his property, and his sacred honor; —let every man remember that to violate the law, is to trample on the blood of his father, and to tear the character of his own, and his children's liberty. Let reverence for the laws, be breathed by every American mother, to the lisping babe, that prattles on her lap—let it be taught in schools, in seminaries, and in colleges; —let it be written in Primers, spelling books, and in Almanacs; —let it be preached from the pulpit, proclaimed in legislative halls, and enforced in courts of justice. And, in short, let it become the political religion of the nation; and let the old and the young, the rich and the poor, the grave and the gay, of all sexes and tongues, and colors and conditions, sacrifice unceasingly upon its altars...

【Question】

What is the main idea of this paragraph?

A) It emphasizes the idea that everyone should follow the laws.

B) It shows that American people usually break the laws.

C) It explains why people should not violate the laws.

D) It challenges a widely-held view of the laws.

【解析】这个段落主要是排比，所以这种段落基本上可以通过第一句判断重要观点——不应该违反法律，所以答案选 A。

例 4

Antipathy is the only word which can express the feeling Edward Crimsworth had for me—a feeling, in a great measure, involuntary, and which was liable to be excited by every, the most trifling movement, look, or word of mine. My southern accent annoyed him; the degree of education evinced in my language irritated him; my punctuality, industry, and accuracy, fixed his dislike, and gave it the high flavour and poignant relish of envy; he feared that I too should one day make a successful tradesman. Had I been in anything inferior to him, he would not have hated me so thoroughly, but I knew all that he knew, and, what was worse, he suspected that I kept the padlock of silence on mental wealth in which he was no sharer. If he could have once placed me in a ridiculous or mortifying position, he would have forgiven me much, but I was guarded by three faculties—Caution, Tact, Observation; and prowling and prying as was Edward's malignity, it could never baffle the lynx-eyes of these, my natural sentinels. Day by day did his malice watch my tact, hoping it would sleep, and prepared to steal snake-like on its slumber; but tact, if it be genuine, never sleeps.

同理，这个段落中也没有转折句。所以第一句概括了段落的主要内容。

Most people know the gruesome story of Baron Victor Frankenstein, the arrogant doctor who created a living creature from the bodies of corpses, only to see his creation turn murderous. The story has been told and retold. It has also been the subject of numerous films, and most people are familiar with the tale, so much so that we use allusions, or references, to Frankenstein's monster to describe a good idea gone very wrong. What many people don't know, however, is that the chilling story of Dr. Frankenstein and his creature was written by a nineteen-year-old newlywed named Mary Shelley. As a young bride, Shelley liked to take part in storytelling competitions with her husband. On one particularly long evening in 1816, her husband Byron suggested that everyone compose a ghost story. In response to Byron's suggestion, Mary Shelley spent the night writing and was ready the next day with the story of Dr. Frankenstein, the man who constructed a creature from body parts and galvanized it into action. When she read it aloud, everyone agreed Shelley's story was the best by far, and by 1818 she had published it as a novel.

【Question】

What is the main idea of this paragraph?

A) It indicates that Mary Shelly was a famous writer.

B) It contrasts the popularity of a book and the fame of its author.

C) It illustrates that Frankenstein is a ghost story.

D. It explains why a book is well-known.

【解析】这个段落的主要句子是出现在中间的转折句，该句说大多数人并不熟悉这部小说的作者。所以答案选择 B——对比这本书的流行和其作者的名声。

例 6

Reduction in numbers of game should have boded ill for their survival in later times. A worsening of the plight of deer was to be expected as settlers encroached on the land, logging, burning, and clearing, eventually replacing a wilderness landscape with roads, cities, towns, and factories. No doubt the numbers of deer declined still further. Recall the fate of the Columbian white-tailed deer, now in a protected status. But for the black-tailed deer, human pressure has had just the opposite effect. Wildlife zoologist Helmut Buechner (1953), in reviewing the nature of biotic changes in Washington through recorded time, says that "since the early 1940s, the state has had more deer than at any other time in its history, the winter population fluctuating around approximately 320,000 deer (mule and black-tailed deer), which will yield about 65,000 of either sex and any age annually for an indefinite period."

【Question】

What is the main purpose of this paragraph?

A) To provide support for the idea that habitat destruction would lead to population decline

B) To compare how two species of deer caused biotic changes in the wilderness environment

C) To contrast the different impacts that humans exert on deer.

D) To argue that some deer species must be given a protected status

【解析】这个段落仍然是对比，中间出现重要的对比逻辑，对比的是人类对不同鹿的影响是不一样的。所以答案选 C。

本章练习与答案解析

一、本章练习题

练习 1: 寻找细节——从下面题目的选项中找到与题干对应的细节信息

题 1

Some people just will not believe that Elvis is dead.

A) Decades after his death, websites with names like "Elvis Lives" report sightings of the man once called the "King of Rock and Roll."

B) Sting, Sheryl Crow, and Justin Timberlake are just a few of the musicians who have said Elvis was a big influence on their music.

题 2

The Roman Empire was a victim of its own success.

A) As time went on, the Romans were unable to control the territories they had conquered, and the empire did not have enough soldiers to suppress rebellions.

B) The Romans were known for being cruel to the inhabitants of the territories they conquered.

题 3

Many well-known writers are in the habit of re-reading their favorite books.

A) J. K. Rowling, the author of the *Harry Potter* books, told Oprah Winfrey that her favorite book was *The Woman Who Walked into Doors*, a novel about a woman in an abusive relationship.

B) Best-selling writer Stephen King has read *Lord of the Flies* at least three times.

题 4

Pit bulls are not, by nature, vicious dogs, who attack for no reason; their reputation is undeserved.

A) Before pit bulls were trained as fight dogs by being subjected to repeated abuse and cruelty, they were considered the ideal family pets due to their loyal and gentle nature.

B) People who are convicted of breeding and training pit bulls to fight one another should be sent to jail for a minimum of five years.

C) The poet and philosopher Vicki Hearne spent her life defending the rights of animals, using her poetry and prose to express her belief that animals are capable of both compassion and loyalty.

题 5

Despite strong security efforts, pirates have become bolder in their attacks on vessels sailing off the African coast.

A) Pirates attack private boats in the hope of taking prisoners who can be held for ransom.

B) Pirates have increased attacks off the coast of East Africa in recent years despite an international flotilla of warships dedicated to protecting vessels and stopping the pirate assaults.

C) The government of Somalia is barely functioning, which is one of the reasons the waters off the coast of Somalia are a hot spot for pirate attacks.

练习 2: 画线标记段落中的重要信息并注意阅读速度的变化

题 1

Although oil and gasoline remain important energy sources, it is natural gas that currently supplies around 25 percent of America's energy needs. A recent study shows that natural gas use was roughly 22 trillion cubic feet (TCF) annually. Natural gas demand is increasing at phenomenal rates because of its ability to create cleaner fuel for electrical power. Experts predict that annual demand is likely to increase to almost 32 TCF in less than a decade. At a consumption rate of 32 TCF per year, the United States would only have about a five-year supply of natural gas. Known natural gas reserves in North America are quickly becoming exhausted. In fact, in the past thirty years, known supplies have dwindled from almost 300 TCF to around 150 TCF.

题 2

It doesn't have to be like this. Done right, public transport can be faster, more comfortable, and cheaper than the private automobile. In Shanghai, German-made magnetic levitation trains skim over elevated tracks at 266 miles an hour, whisking people to the airport at a third of the speed of sound. In provincial French towns, electric-powered streetcars run silently on rubber tires, sliding through narrow streets along a single guide rail set into cobblestones. From Spain to Sweden, Wi-Fi equipped high-speed trains seamlessly connect with highly ramified metro networks, allowing commuters to work on laptops as they prepare for same-day meetings in once distant capital cities. In Latin America, China, and India, working people board fast-loading buses that move like subway trains along dedicated busways, leaving the sedans and SUVs of the rich mired in dawn-to-dusk traffic jams. And some cities have transformed their streets into cycle-path freeways, making giant strides in public health and safety and the sheer livability of their neighborhoods—in the process turning the workaday bicycle into a viable form of mass transit.

题 3

Ken settled on the Chukar Partridge as a model species, but he might not have made his discovery without a key piece of advice from the local rancher in Montana who was supplying him with birds. When the cowboy stopped by to see how things were going, Ken showed him his nice, tidy laboratory setup and explained how the birds' first hops and flights would be measured. The rancher was incredulous. "He took one look and said, in pretty colorful language, 'What are those birds doing on the ground? They hate to be on the ground! Give them something to climb on!'" At first it seemed unnatural—ground birds don't like the ground? But as he thought about it Ken realized that all the species he'd watched in the wild preferred to rest on ledges, low branches, or other elevated perches where they were safe from predators. They really only used the ground for feeding and traveling. So he brought in some hay bales for the Chukars to perch on and then left his son in charge of feeding and data collection while he went away on a short work trip.

He and others note that the bias against null studies can waste time and money when researchers devise new studies replicating strategies already found to be ineffective. Worse, if researchers publish significant results from similar experiments in the future, they could look stronger than they should because the earlier null studies are ignored. Even more troubling to Malhotra was the fact that two scientists whose initial studies "didn't work out" went on to publish results based on a smaller sample. "The non-TESS version of the same study, in which we used a student sample, did yield fruit," noted one investigator.

Serious coverage of goings-on in government is deterred by the fact that government is so technical that even career civil servants cannot explain what is happening. In 1978 I attended a seminar on federal estate and gift tax, where the Internal Revenue Service lawyers responsible for this area frankly confessed that they did not understand the Tax Reform Act of 1976. Intricate technical issues such as taxation, arms control, and nuclear power are difficult to understand for professionals, to say nothing of the most diligent layman.

练习 3: 段落概要 / 目的题

There is yet another approach: instead of rooting ethics in character or the consequences of actions, we can focus on our actions themselves. From this perspective some things are right, some wrong—we should buy fair trade goods, we shouldn't tell lies in advertisements. Ethics becomes a list of commandments, a catalog of "dos" and "dont's." When a finance official refuses to devalue a currency because they have promised not to, they are defining ethics this way. According to this approach devaluation can still be bad, even if it would make everybody better off.

The main purpose of the fifth paragraph (lines 45—56) is to

A) develop a counterargument to the claim that greed is good.

B) provide support for the idea that ethics is about character.

C) describe a third approach to defining ethical economics.

D) illustrate that one's actions are a result of one's character.

Some of the largest ocean waves in the world are nearly impossible to see. Unlike other large waves, these rollers, called internal waves, do not ride the ocean surface. Instead, they move underwater, undetectable without the use of satellite imagery or sophisticated monitoring equipment. Despite their hidden nature, internal waves are fundamental parts of ocean water dynamics, transferring heat to the ocean depths and bringing up cold water from below. And they can reach staggering heights-some as tall as skyscrapers.

The first paragraph serves mainly to

A) explain how a scientific device is used.

B) note a common misconception about an event.

C) describe a natural phenomenon and address its importance.

D) Present a recent study and summarize its findings.

This hypothesis can best be tested by a trial wherein a small number of commercial honey bee colonies are offered a number of pyrethrum producing plants, as well as a typical bee food source such as clover, while controls are offered only the clover. Mites could then be introduced to each hive with note made as to the choice of the bees, and the effects of the mite parasites on the experimental colonies versus control colonies.

The main purpose of the fourth paragraph (lines 42—50) is to

A) summarize the results of an experiment that confirmed the authors' hypothesis about the role of clover in the diets of wild-type honeybees.

B) propose an experiment to investigate how different diets affect commercial honeybee colonies' susceptibility to mite infestations.

C) provide a comparative nutritional analysis of the honey produced by the experimental colonies and by the control colonies.

D) predict the most likely outcome of an unfinished experiment summarized in the third paragraph (ines19-41).

The Alcazar Restaurant was on Sheridan Road near Devon Avenue. It was long and narrow, with tables for two along the walls and tables for four down the middle. The decoration was art *moderne*, except for the series of murals depicting the four seasons, and the sick ferns in the front window. Lymie sat down at the second table from the cash register, and ordered his dinner. The history book, which he propped against the catsup and the glass sugar bowl, had been used by others before him. Blank pages front and back were filled in with maps, drawings, dates, comic cartoons, and organs of the body; also with names and messages no longer clear and never absolutely legible. On nearly every other page there was some marginal notation, either in ink or in very hard pencil. And unless someone had upset a glass of water, the marks on page 177 were from tears.

The main purpose of the first paragraph is to

A) introduce the passage's main character by showing his nightly habits.

B) indicate the date the passage takes place by presenting period details.

C) convey the passage's setting by describing a place and an object.

D) foreshadow an event that is described in detail later in the passage.

But there was one telling difference between the brains of the mental athletes and the control subjects; When the researchers looked at which parts of the brain were lighting up when the mental athletes were memorizing, they found that they were activating entirely different circuitry. According to the functional MRIS (fMRIs), regions of the brain that were less active in the control subjects seemed to be working in overdrive for the mental athletes.

The main purpose of the fifth paragraph (lines 57—65) is to

A) relate Maguires study of mental athletes to her study of taxi drivers.

B) speculate on the reason for Maguire’s unexpected results.

C) identify an important finding of maguire’s study of mental athletes.

D) transition from a summary of maguire’s findings to a description of her methods.

Another man might have thrown up his hands—but not Nawabdin. His twelve daughters acted as a spur to his genius, and he looked with satisfaction in the mirror each morning at the face of a warrior going out to do battle. Nawab of course knew that he must proliferate his sources of revenue—the salary he received from K. K. Harouni for tending the tube wells would not even begin to suffice. He set up a little one-room flour mill, run off a condemned electric motor—condemned by him. He tried his hand at fish-farming in a little pond at the edge of his master’s fields. He bought broken radios, fixed them, and resold them. He did not demur even when asked to fix watches, though that enterprise did spectacularly badly, and in fact earned him more kicks than kudos, for no watch he took apart ever kept time again.

The main purpose of the first paragraph is to

A) characterize Nawab as a loving father.

B) outline the schedule of a typical day in Nawab's life.

C) describe Nawab's various moneymaking ventures.

D) contrast Nawab's and harouni's lifestyles.

题 7

Scientists do not know how the birds find that aerodynamic sweet spot, but they suspect that the animals align themselves either by sight or by sensing air currents through their feathers. Alternatively, they may move around until they find the location with the least resistance. In future studies, the researchers will switch to more common birds, such as pigeons or geese. They plan to investigate how the animals decide who sets the course and the pace, and whether a mistake made by the leader can ripple through the rest of the flock to cause traffic jams.

What is a main idea of the seventh paragraph (ines62–73)?

A) Different types of hierarchies exist in each flock of birds.

B) Mistakes can happen when long-winged birds create a V formation.

C) Future research will help scientists to better understand V formations.

D) Long-winged birds watch the lead bird closely to keep a V formation intact.

二、答案与解析

练习 1 答案

答案选 A。

答案选 A。

题 3

答案选 B。

题 4

答案选 A。

题 5

答案选 B。

练习 2 答案

Although oil and gasoline remain important energy sources, it is natural gas that currently supplies around 25 percent of America's energy needs. A recent study shows that natural gas use was roughly 22 trillion cubic feet (TCF) annually. Natural gas demand is increasing at phenomenal rates because of its ability to create cleaner fuel for electrical power. Experts predict that annual demand is likely to increase to almost 32 TCF in less than a decade. At a consumption rate of 32 TCF per year, the United States would only have about a five-year supply of natural gas. Known natural gas reserves in North America are quickly becoming exhausted. In fact, in the past thirty years, known supplies have dwindled from almost 300 TCF to around 150 TCF.

题 2

It doesn't have to be like this. Done right, public transport can be faster, more comfortable, and cheaper than the private automobile.In Shanghai, German-made magnetic levitation trains skim over elevated tracks at 266 miles an hour, whisking people to the airport at a third of the speed of sound. In provincial French towns, electric-powered streetcars run silently on rubber tires, sliding through narrow streets along a single guide rail set into cobblestones. From Spain to Sweden, Wi-Fi equipped high-speed trains seamlessly connect with highly ramified metro networks, allowing commuters to work on laptops as they prepare for same-day meetings in once distant capital cities. In Latin America, China, and India, working people board fast-loading buses that move like subway trains along dedicated busways, leaving the sedans and SUVs of the rich mired in dawn-to-dusk traffic jams. And some cities have transformed their streets into cycle-path freeways, making giant strides in public health and safety and the sheer livability of their neighborhoods—in the process turning the workaday bicycle into a viable form of mass transit.

题 3

Ken settled on the Chukar Partridge as a model species, but he might not have made his discovery without a key piece of advice from the local rancher in Montana who was supplying him with birds. When the cowboy stopped by to see how things were going, Ken showed him his nice, tidy laboratory setup and explained how the birds' first hops and flights would be measured. The rancher was incredulous. "He took one look and said, in pretty colorful language, 'What are those birds doing on the ground? They hate to be on the ground! Give them something to climb on!'" At first it seemed unnatural—ground birds don't like the ground? But as he thought about it Ken realized that all the species he'd watched in the wild preferred to rest on ledges, low branches, or other elevated perches where they were safe from predators. They really only used the ground for feeding and traveling. So he brought in some hay bales for the Chukars to perch on and then left his son in charge of feeding and data collection while he went away on a short work trip

题 4

He and others note that the bias against null studies can waste time and money when researchers devise new studies replicating strategies already found to be ineffective. Worse, if researchers publish significant results from similar experiments in the future, they could look stronger than they should because the earlier null studies are ignored. Even more troubling to Malhotra was the fact that two scientists whose initial studies "didn't work out" went on to publish results based on a smaller sample. "The non-TESS version of the same study, in which we used a student sample, did yield fruit," noted one investigator.

题 5

Serious coverage of goings-on in government is deterred by the fact that government is so technical that even career civil servants cannot explain what is happening. In 1978 I attended a seminar on federal estate and gift tax, where the Internal Revenue Service lawyers responsible for this area frankly confessed that they did not understand the Tax Reform Act of 1976. Intricate technical issues such as taxation, arms control, and nuclear power are difficult to understand for professionals, to say nothing of the most diligent layman.

练习 3 答案与解析

题 1

答案选 C。

【解析】这个段落最重要的句子是 "There is yet another approach: instead of rooting ethics in character or the consequences of actions, wecan focus on our actions themselves."，而后面都是细节呈现。通过这个句子可以知道整个段落重心放在另外一种方法上，就是关注行为本身，而不用关注性格或是行为带来的结果。

A 错误，因为并不是 greed is good 的相反观点，只是另外一种理解方法。

B 错误，因为并不是继续讲解性格问题。

D 错误，因为并不是想展示人的行为是性格的结果。

题 2

答案选 C。

【解析】这个段落最重要的句子是“Some of the largest ocean waves in the world are nearly impossible to see.”，这句话引出文章的话题 internalwaves，之后讲解 internalwaves 的各类细节，比如在海平面之下、肉眼看不到以及深度。

A 错误，话题不是科学仪器。

B 错误，并未提及任何错误概念。

D 错误，并未提及任何研究或成果。

题 3

答案选 B。

【解析】段落中最重要的信息是“This hypothesis can best be tested by a trial”（这个假设可以被一个实验所测试）。后面都是通过具体信息来说明实验的设置。所以段落目的就是通过实验而验证某个假设。

A 错误，并非实验结果。

C 错误，并非为了研究蜂蜜的营养。

D 错误，并非预测任何东西。

题 4

答案选 C。

【解析】段落中最重要的概念首先是第一句的“the Alcazar Restaurant”，之后写这个餐厅的细节（布局、桌椅、装饰）；其次是第 8 行的“the history book”，之后描述这本书的细节。所以第一段就是描写餐厅和书；餐厅是 place，地点；书是 object，物品。整个都是 setting，小说的环境或是场景。

A 错误，并未提及 nightly habits。

B 错误，主要目的不是说明文章发生的时间。

D 错误，没有预示任何事情的发生。

题 5

答案选 C。

【解析】段落最重要句子是首句中的“there was one telling difference”，后面都是对区别的具体描述，所以段落的作用是呈现实验的一个结果，即 important finding。

A 错误，并非联系两个研究。

B 错误，并不是猜想原因。

D 错误，并没有转折。

题 6

答案选 C。

【解析】文章首先引出主要人物——Nawabdin，他把自己当做是勇士一样去赚更多的钱，来养活自己的 12 个女儿。而后文主要是介绍他做了哪些事情去赚钱，用排比的手法展现：He set up...He tried...He did not demur... 所以整个段落主要说明 Nawabdin 赚钱的方式。

A 错误，并非具体描述他如何 loving。

B 错误，并非 typical day（典型一天）的事情安排。

D 错误，没有对比两个人的生活方式。

题 7

答案选 C。

【解析】这个段落主要是讲科学家其实并不清楚这些鸟如何找到空气动力学非常“甜美”的地方。之后提出了一些猜想并说明后续可以做什么来去解决这个疑问。

A 错误，并非讨论鸟类的等级制度。

B 错误，并非讨论鸟类犯的错误。

D 错误，这是一个细节， 并非段落概要或目的。

第四章

词汇题的破解之道

SAT SAT SAT SAT SAT SAT SAT SAT SAT SAT SAT SAT SAT SAT SAT SAT SAT

在2016年SAT改革之后，新SAT阅读板块对词汇的测试从过去的生僻词（老SAT的Sentence Completion）转到了词汇的语境（Context）意思考查。根据SAT官方指南的描述，考查的词汇更多的是实用性强的学术词汇或词组（high-utility academic words and phrases）。从这点上来说，新SAT的改革确实更加贴近美国大学的学习要求。新SAT的词汇题考查的是学生精准理解一个单词/词组在特定语境中的含义。

那么到底何为语境?

语境，直白点说就是上下文或者语言使用的环境。一个单词在不同的上下文当中意思其实不一样，比如bank这个大家都熟悉的单词。

He went to the bank to draw some money.

He was walking alone on the bank.

这两句话中都有bank，但是很明显上句的bank意思为“银行”，下句的bank意思为“河岸”。不只是单词在不同语境中意思不一样，一句话在不同的语境中意思也会截然不同。比如对“今天天气好吗？”这样简单一句话的理解。

语境1：周末的清晨，小A同学早早起床吃了早饭。看到窗外阳光明媚，他决定打电话邀请同学小B一起去打球。小B同学被手机铃声叫醒，睡眼惺忪地问道：“今天天气好吗？”

语境2：在一个寒冬的夜晚，外面下着阴冷的小雨。小A百无聊赖地坐在客厅沙发上，转过头对旁边的小B说，“我们出去逛街吧。”小B惊讶地看着小A，“外面天气好吗？”

大家很容易判断出来，在语境1中，那句话的意思是小B不知道外面天气怎么样，所以提出疑问；而在语境2中，小B其实是不想出去逛街，通过反问和质疑说明自己不想出去逛街。

在新SAT中，对单词的语境理解考查也是占有很大比重的，在15%左右。我们来看一下2016—2017年部分试题中的词汇题比例。

官方真题	词汇题数量	占比
2016年3月北美	8	15%
2016年5月亚洲	8	15%
2016年6月亚洲	9	17%
2016年10月亚洲	7	13%
2016年11月亚洲	8	15%
2016年12月亚洲	7	13%
2016年1月北美	8	15%
2016年5月亚洲	8	15%

词汇题做题思路

代入原文，确定准确意思——SAT 的词汇题，不像托福的词汇题，认识就可以直接选择，而是应该看这个单词在原文语境中的意思。所以一定不要觉得自己认识就直接挑选答案。比如我们看下一道托福的词汇题和一道 SAT 的词汇题。

The word “**methods**” in the passage is closest in meaning to

○ ways

○ shades

○ stages

○ rules

这道题考查的是 methods，大家肯定都知道是“方法”的意思，所以直接选 ways。

As used in line 24, “**common**” most nearly means

A) numerous.

B) familiar.

C) widespread.

D) ordinary.

这个题目，大家肯定知道 common 的意思，“普通的，平常的”。那么可以直接选 ordinary 么？不可以！我们来看一下原文。

The production, circulation, and reception of public knowledge is a complex process. It is generally accepted that public knowledge should be authoritative, but there is not always common agreement about what the public needs to know, who is best placed to relate and explain it, and how authoritative reputations should be determined and evaluated. Historically, newspapers such as *The*

所以，在这里，there is not always common agreement about... 的意思是关于某件事情，大家没有一个 common 一致意见。所以 common 在这里修饰 agreement，表示大家可能并没有都“广泛”同意的观点，而不是“普通的”一致意见。答案选 widespread。

作答 **SAT** 词汇题的具体方法。

(1) 词性判断

考试中常考的词性有：名词 (*n*)、动词 (*v*)、形容词 (*adj*)、副词 (*adv*)。可以从语法角度对词性进行判断，看单词在句子中充当的成分即可。

No ostentation; for how could it survive, when there was nothing left of Fauntleroy, **save** penury and shame!

save 通常作动词，意为“拯救，救助”。但是在这个句子中 save 不是动词，不然语法上是不通的，可以判断出来是介词，意思根据语境可以推出是“除了”。所以如果出 save 的词汇题，应该选择 except 或其他近义词选项。

(2) 作用判断

对某个单词的词性确定之后，我们就可以根据词性来判断其作用。假设这个单词是形容词，那么其作用肯定是修饰或描述某个名词；若这个单词是副词，那么其作用是修饰某个动词或形容词，或者修饰整个句子。根据修饰的成分或者搭配就可以确定或排除一些选项。

The hymn was written by an **obscure** Greek composer.

这句话中的 obscure 可以判断为形容词，修饰 composer (作曲家)。obscure 这个单词虽然经常表示“模糊不清的”，但如果选项中有 unclear 和 unknown，应该选择 unknown (不出名的，不被人所知的)，因为“不清晰的作曲家”显然搭配不当。

(3) 正负面判断

这是非常实用的方法。大多数单词从情感上可以分为正面、负面和中性。如果通过文章的语境和语气可以推出正负面的话，那么选项就很好选择了。比如：

Reality TV shows will **adversely** affect traditional dramas and comedies. As reality TV increases in popularity, network executives will begin canceling more traditional dramas and comedies and replacing them with the latest in reality TV.

A) mildly B) kindly C) negatively D) immediately

思路：adversely，副词，修饰 affect；通过句子可以判断为负面情感 (后面说是取消了很多传统戏剧和喜剧，所以真人秀节目对传统节目的影响是负面的)。所以直接选择 negatively，其他选项均为正面或中性情感。

(4) 抽象、具体判断

抽象 (abstract)，字面意思，形象被抽掉了，就剩下一个概念。abstract 也有“提取，分离”的意思。我们把很多类似的具体东西集结起来，抽出它们本质的东西，忽略其他部分，就是抽象了。而具体 (concrete、specific) 指的是“细节的，明确的，真实存在的”。比如朋友 (friend)

是很具体的，但是友谊 (friendship) 就比较抽象了。比如：

When in the course of human events, it becomes necessary for one people to dissolve the **bands** which have connected them with another, and to assume among the earth, the separate and equal **station** to which the Laws of Nature and of Nature`s God entitle them, a decent respect to the opinions of mankind required that they should declare the causes which compel them to the separation.

bands 的常见意思为“带，乐队”，但是在这里其意思是抽象的，表示“关系，关联”，如果出词汇题，选项应该类似 connection；station 的常见意思为“车站”，在这里表示“地位”，如果出词汇题，选项应该是 status。

(5) 近义词、反义词寻找

经常在原文中会出现被考查单词的近义词、反义词，大家可以根据原文的逻辑关系判断是近义词还是反义词。通常并列 / 递进 / 因果关系是近义词；而转折 / 对比关系是反义词。比如：

Mr. Healey was obviously guilty of **nepotism** when he promoted his twenty-two-year-old son to district manager: many other employees were better qualified for the position.

暗含因果关系，Mr. Healey 把自己的儿子提拔为经理，所以有 nepotism 的罪恶感，因为其他员工更有资格。所以这里说的是利用职权谋私，故 nepotism 的意思可以猜测出来为“偏袒，裙带关系”

The large, luxurious homes and spacious, well-tended lawns made it obvious that people of considerable **affluence** lived in this area.

（暗含因果关系，因为这个地方是 large、luxurious，所以住在这个地方的人是“富裕的”）

I thought Meredith would be eager to talk about her new job, but she showed complete **apathy** when I asked her about it.

（转折关系，apathy 和 be eager to talk 相反，所以 apathy 意为“冷漠”）

Posthumously, Van Gogh is recognized as one of the world's greatest artists, but this certainly was not the case during his lifetime.

（对比关系，凡高 posthumously 被大家认为是世界上最伟大的艺术家之一，但在其生前并不是这样。所以 posthumously 意为“逝世后”）

词汇题错误主要原因汇总

尽管上面我们详细讲解了如何作答词汇题，但是大家还是容易做错。如果词汇题做错，主要原因有三。

1. 做题不按照思路，全凭感觉

这点比较容易解决，就是把上面的做题思路认真研究一下。

2. 虽然按照思路做题，但是先入为主

先入为主的错误经常表现为学生认识这个单词，会自然地倾向于选择这个单词的常见近义词。虽然后面还会在文章中结合语境思考，但是因为已经先入为主，所以即使看过文章和经过后续的思考也不能改变其对答案的选择。比如：

Many of the proteins that our cells crank out naturally make for good medicine. Our bodies' own enzymes, hormones, clotting factors, and antibodies are commonly used to treat cancer, diabetes, autoimmune diseases, and more. The trouble is that it's difficult and expensive to make these compounds on an industrial scale, and as a result, patients can face shortages of the medicines they need. Dairy animals, on the other hand, are **expert** protein producers, their udders swollen with milk. So the creation of the first transgenic animals—first mice,then other species—in the 1980s gave scientists an idea: What if they put the gene for a human antibody or enzyme into a cow, goat, or sheep?

As used in the paragraph, "expert" most nearly means

A) knowledgeable.　　B) professional.　　C) capable.　　D) trained.

这道题很多同学会选择 B 选项 professional，主要原因就是因为认识 expert，认为其意思是"专家"，很简单啊。于是看到选项 professional，内心其实早已先入为主，总觉得这个选项最好。至于之后看不看文章或是想不想我们前面介绍的五种方法都不重要了。因为即使经过思考也会努力说服自己之前的选择是正确的。

其实这道题应该选择 C 选项 "capable"。因为这里的 expert 在文章中（或者根据选项来看）是形容词，是用来修饰动物的。所以选项中能够修饰动物，而且表达产生蛋白质的能力很强的，肯定就是 capable 了。

再比如：

Smith's team began to test the cockatoos' learning process to **discern** whether and to what extent the birds in their study could solve all five puzzles without intermittent rewards.

As used in the sentence, "discern" most nearly means

A) determine　　B) notice　　C) challenge　　D) differentiate

这道题很多同学会选择 D，因为 discern 最常见的意思就是"区分，辨别"。而且考生如果认识这个词甚至感觉还蛮好的，还挺骄傲的，说明自己单词背得好。于是就先入为主地去看文章了。看完文章觉得懂了，这个小组就是想区分鸟的学习能力，说得通。

但是，错了。因为根据文章句子意思，这个小组是想 ________ 这些鸟是否能够以及解决这些 puzzle 的能力到达什么程度而去做这个实验。那么空格填什么词最适合？肯定填"确定"最好：确定这些鸟是否有能力以及其能力达到什么程度，而不是为了区分任何东西，所以答案为 A 选项 determine。

3. 选项单词不认识

这种情况其实在考试时候没有很好的办法解决，因为假设四个单词中有两个不认识，而正好正确选项不认识，那么确实没有办法确保一定能做对。所以唯一能够做的就是在平时提升自己的词汇量。

一、思路练习题

题 1

Although social work is not a particularly **lucrative** career, I wouldn't do anything else. Knowing I'm helping others is far more important to me than money.

A) profitable B) exciting C) rewarding D) embarrassing

题 2

When you are in an interview, try not to show any overt signs that you are **nervous**.

A) essential B) uneasy C) obvious D) ambiguous

题 3

Jack became intensely **acerbic** and began to cruelly and vindictively make fun of all his buddies.

A) bitter B) adept C) compliant D) benign

题 4

Intolerant people tend to disdain all those who **disagree** with them

A) appreciate B) upset C) scorn D) conceal

题 5

To elude capture, the clever criminals **waded** into the river and floated with the logs.

A) adorn B) express C) fight D) escape

题 6

When invasive species come into any area, the **indigenous** life forms will be threatened

A) lazy B) weak C) native D) vivid

题 7

That **compelling** the colonies to pay money without their consent would be rather like raising contributions in an enemy's country.

A) captivating B) forcing C) connecting D) alluring

二、真题练习题

(2016 年 5 月北美 Practice Test 5)

题 1

The young man had never for one second deserted Mr. Peters. He was always there, tugging at Mr. Peters' elbow, making him do things that were not **becoming** in a man of forty-five.

A) emerging B) fitting C) developing D) happening

题 2

Heaven has appointed to one sex the superior, and to the other the subordinate **station**, and this without any reference to the character or conduct of either.

A) region B) studio C) district D) rank

题 3

But it was designed that the mode of gaining influence and of exercising power should be altogether different and **peculiar**...

A) eccentric B) surprising C) distinctive D) infrequent

题 4

Conventional industrial agriculture has become incredibly efficient on a **simple** land to food basis. Thanks to fertilizers, mechanization and irrigation, each American farmer feeds over 155 people worldwide.

A) straightforward B) modest C) unadorned D) easy

题 5

Today's organic farming practices are probably best deployed in fruit and vegetable farms, where growing nutrition (not just bulk calories) is the primary goal. But for delivering **sheer** calories, especially in our staple crops of wheat, rice, maize, soybeans and so on, conventional farms have the advantage right now.

A) transparent B) abrupt C) steep D) pure

题 6

Will companies be able to **boost** their products by manipulating online ratings on a massive scale? "That is easier said than done," Watts says. If people detect—or learn—that comments on a website are being manipulated, the herd may spook and leave entirely.

A) increase　　B) accelerate　　C) promote　　D) protect

题 7

Will companies be able to boost their products by manipulating online ratings on a massive **scale**? "That is easier said than done," Watts says. If people detect—or learn—that comments on a website are being manipulated, the herd may spook and leave entirely.

A) level　　B) wage　　C) interval　　D) scheme

题 8

It had long been thought that the adult brain was incapable of spawning new neurons—that while learning caused synapses to rearrange themselves and new links between brain cells to form, the brain's **basic** anatomical structure was more or less static. Maguire's study suggested the old inherited wisdom was simply not true.

A) initial　　B) simple　　C) necessary　　D) fundamental

题 9

The researchers put both the mental athletes and a group of **matched** control subjects into MRI scanners and asked them to memorize three-digit numbers, black-and-white photographs of people's faces, and magnified images of snowflakes, while their brains were being scanned.

A) comparable　　B) identical　　C) distinguishable　　D) competing

二、练习题答案

1. 思路练习题答案

题 1

答案选 A。

题 2

答案选 B。

题 3

答案选 A。

题 4

答案选 C。

题 5

答案选 D。

题 6

答案选 C。

题 7

答案选 B。

2. 真题练习题答案

题 1

答案选 B。

题 2

答案选 D。

题 3

答案选 C。

题 4

答案选 A。

题 5

答案选 D。

题 6

答案选 C。

题 7

答案选 A。

题 8

答案选 D。

题 9

答案选 A。

第五章

句子作用和目的题

句子的作用

大多数同学在阅读的时候只关注句子的意思，甚至只是字面意思，而忽略了句子的作用。所谓句子的作用，就是撇开句子的字面意思，研究句子在上下文中对于段落的展开或是传达作者意图所起到的作用。

句子的意思和作用是两个不同的概念；有时候理解了句子可能不是很清楚句子的作用，反之亦然。那么句子通常有哪些作用呢？

我们首先给大家看一个例子。

Black holes are the most efficient engines of destruction known to humanity. Their intense gravity is a one-way ticket to oblivion, and materials spiraling into them can be heat up to millions of degrees and glow brightly. Yet, they are not all powerful. Even super massive black holes are miniscule cosmic standards. They typically account for less than one percent of their galaxy's mass. Accordingly, astronomers have long assumed that super massive black holes, let alone their smaller cousins, would have had little effect beyond their immediate neighborhoods. So it has become as surprise over the past decade that black hole activity is closely intertwined with star formation occurring farther out in the galaxy.

大家首先理解一下这些句子的意思，然后可以思考下每句话的作用。

	Sentence	意思	作用
1	Black holes are the most efficient engines of destruction known to humanity.	黑洞是人类所知晓的最有破坏力的东西。	提出一种说法 / 观点 (present a claim)
2	Their intense gravity is a one-way ticket to oblivion, and materials spiraling into them can be heat up to millions of degrees and glow brightly.	黑洞的巨大引力具有非常强的摧毁力，任何物质只要卷入进去，温度就会达到几百万度，然后被燃烧掉。	具体描述有什么破坏力 (illustrate the previous claim with detail)
3	Yet, they are not all powerful.	但是，它们也不是全能的。	提出转折 (present a transition)
4—5	Even super massive black holes are miniscule cosmic standards. They typically account for less than one percent of their galaxy's mass.	即使是超级大的黑洞按照宇宙的标准也是很小的；它们占到其星系总质量的不到1%。	解释为什么不是全能的 (show explanations)

6	Accordingly, astronomers have long assumed that super massive black holes, let alone their smaller cousins, would have had little effect beyond their immediate neighborhoods.	所以，长期以来，天文学家怀有这种假设——超级黑洞（不用说更小的黑洞了）对它们“邻居”之外的影响是微乎其微的。	得出一个推论（draw a hypothesis）
7	So it has become as surprise over the past decade that black hole activity is closely intertwined with star formation occurring farther out in the galaxy.	在过去十年，发现黑洞活动和很远地方的星球形成都有紧密关联的时候，大家是非常惊讶的。	用事实反驳之前的推论（contradict the hypothesis）

如果我们把以上句子的作用整合一下，就构成这篇短文章的行文思路（passage development）或者说文章结构（passage structure）。

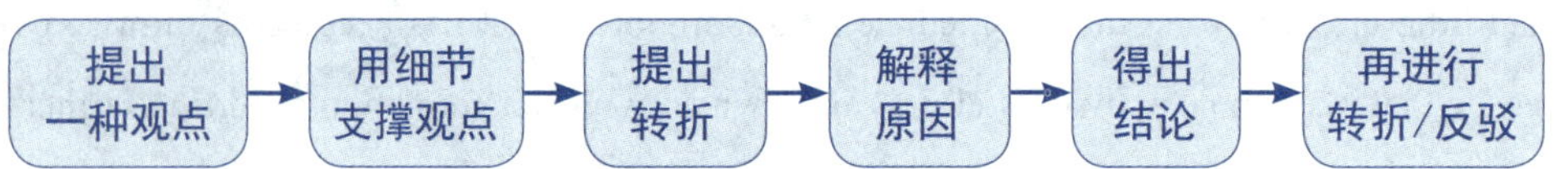

一、句子作用

在 SAT 考试中，句子的常见作用有 20 多种，这里给大家做个汇总。

1. 引入话题

这种句子通常是描述一种社会现象或发生的事实，或者一个物品、一个概念。比如：

For people with insomnia, they have great difficulty falling asleep. 这里就是引出 insomnia(失眠）的话题。

2. 下定义

对一些普通大众不是很熟悉的概念进行定义或者解释。比如：

Properly speaking, a movement is a collective effort to bring about fundamental social change. 这句话就是给读者定义 movement（运动），而且这里的运动是抽象的运动，而不是具体的物理移动。

3. 提出观点

通常是说出作者的认知和想法，或对某件事情或物体进行评价。比如：

Long-term advertising campaigns are effective to project a solid, enduring image and to maintain an ongoing relationship between consumers and the company's products. 长期的广告活动对于维护客户和公司产品关系是非常有效的。

4. 事实 / 现象描写

完全描写事实或现象，毫无作者的观点或评价。比如：

Women in the 19th century enjoyed fewer rights than men; they were not allowed to participate in the government.

5. 举例、细节描写

通常是对一个整体进行描述或者对某个观点进行细节展开或举例。比如上面这句话中的后半句(they were not allowed to participate in the government)，它既是事实描写，也是对前句(Women in the 19th century enjoyed fewer rights than men) 的细节展开或举例。

6. 转折

通常由 however、yet、nonetheless 引出句子，用于否定或者批判前句。

7. 类比 / 类似

类比的作用是找出共同之处，可以简单理解为 similarity。通常由以下单词 / 短语引出：similarly、along the same lines、just as…、just like…、likewise、in the same way。

8. 对比

和句子前面观点 / 内容相反。比如：

Prior to the nineteenth century, America was a largely agricultural country and daily life required so much effort that there was little time for leisure. **But as industry grew so did city life and leisure time**. 这里第二句和第一句形成了对比关系。

9. 强调

强调的方式有很多种，可以用绝对词 (only、solely、never 等)，也可以使用重复 / 反问等修辞手法，还可以使用表强调语气的单词。比如：

使用绝对词：Only he can truly understand what I feel.

使用反问修辞：Didn't you remember what I told you?

10. 解释

给出对于某种事物 / 观点的原因，也就是为什么出现这样的情况或者为什么持有这样的观点。

11. 结论

结论是从一定的前提推论或者观察得到的结果，以及对事物作出的总结性判断。通常在实验类文章中以 "researchers found that…" "they concluded that" "the results show that…" 等形式出现。

12. 预示

预示指的是预感到即将发生的事情。比如文章开头描写的是一个码头的场景，而后文出现了离别的故事。那么开头的码头场景就是 foreshadow the separation。

13. 提出问题

问题是指某个事物存在的缺陷，需引起大家重视且需要解决的状态。

14. 解决方案

这个和问题是对应的，放在一起就是 problem-solution 的结构。比如：

Problem:

College is a time for accumulation: of knowledge, friends, and experiences. Unfortunately, in the first year, many students also accumulate unwanted weight.

Solution:

Eating too much or not being physically active enough will make one overweight. To maintain one's weight, the calories he/she obtains must equal the energy he/she burns.

15. 呼吁

作者认为某项主张需要大众的支持，而号召人们去干这件事。比如罗斯福总统的一句经典名言：Ask not what your country can do for you; ask what you can do for your country.

16. 让步

当你支持 A 反对 B，行文的时候却阐述 A 的劣势或者 B 的优势，那么就是在让步。比如在讨论纸质文档和电子文档的优劣的时候。

Paper has a unique set of qualities that permit certain kinds of uses. Paper is tangible: we can pick up a document, flip through it, read little bits here and there, and quickly get a sense of it. Paper is spatially flexible, meaning that we can spread it out and arrange it in the way that suits us best. And paper is tailorable: we can easily annotate it, and scribble on it as we read.

Digital documents, of course, have their own advantages. They can easily be searched, shared, stored, and linked to other relevant material.（让步）But they lack the qualities that really matter to a group of people working together on a report.

17. 反驳／质疑

Computer technology was supposed to replace paper.

But that has not happened.（反驳）

Nearly every country in the Western world has seen more paper-use on a per-capita basis.

18. 其他

猜想、列举、排比、悬念、渲染气氛、特点描写、态度回应、警示。

二、练习题

练习 1

Sentence 1: Some people believed that the frequent use of repetition in Native American ceremonial texts was a result of the oral nature and helped make the works easy to remember.

作用：____________________

Sentence 2: However, Native American scholar Paula Allen argues that this factor must be peripheral.

作用：____________________

Sentences 3—4: That is because people in societies without writing have had more finely developed memories that do people who use writing. Native American children learned early to remember complicated instructions and long stories by heart.

作用：____________________

练习 2

(1) For centuries oceanographers have snatched clues to ocean currents where they could.

(2) Early ideas about the speed and direction of currents often came from stray objects that floated and drifted for years.

(3) These days, a host of ingenious instruments delivers intriguing news of the origins and routes of water.

(4) Perhaps the most useful instrument for physical oceanographers is the CTD, which measures the salinity and temperature of a particular mass of seawater at various depths.

What is the function of sentence 3?

练习 3

Sentence 1: Much early childhood literature suggests that the first three years of life are the critical years for brain development.

作用：____________________

Sentence 2: Yet new findings in neuroscience suggest that the brain retains its ability to reorganize itself in response to experience or injury throughout life.

作用：________________

Sentence 3: For example, after the loss of sensory input from an amputated limb, adults are able to learn new motor skills effectively.

作用：________________

Sentence 4: It may be useful to question the simplistic view that the brain becomes unbendable and increasingly difficult to modify beyond the first few years of life.

作用：________________

Sentence 5: If so, we should also be wary of claims that parents have only a single opportunity to help their children build better brains.

作用：________________

练习 4

Sentence 1: Most Americans are accustomed to thinking that lie detectors, because they are machines, can, without error, separate the guilty from the innocent.

作用：________________

Sentence 2: But in fact, lie detectors can and do make mistakes.

作用：________________

Sentence 3: For one thing, those who administer the tests are not necessarily qualified experts.

作用：________________

Sentence 4: Many states don't employ licensed examiners trained to read and interpret lie detector printouts.

作用：________________

Sentence 5: In addition, many subjects react to taking a lie detector test by becoming anxious.

作用：________________

Sentence 6: As a result, their bodies behave as if the subjects were lying even when they are telling the truth.

作用：________________

Sentence 7: Unfortunately, some people are smart enough to use relaxation techniques or tranquilizers to remain calm when they are telling a pack of lies.

作用：________________

练习 5

Sentence 1: There are people in Europe who, confounding together the different characteristics of the sexes, would make of man and woman beings not only equal but alike.

作用：____

Sentence 2: They would give to both the same functions, impose on both the same duties, and grant to both the same rights; they would mix them in all things—their occupations, their pleasures, their business.

作用：____

Sentence 3: It may readily be conceived, that by thus attempting to make one sex equal to the other, both are degraded; and from so preposterous a medley of the works of nature nothing could ever result but weak men and disorderly women

作用：____

三、参考答案

练习 1

Sentence 1 作用：提出观点 (believed)。

Sentence 2 作用：转折 (however)，提出质疑。

Sentences 3—4 作用：给出原因 (because)。

练习 2

Sentence 3 provides a transition (转折)——前面讲的是之前收集洋流数据的方法，从第三句开始是新的方法，之后具体描写是什么方法 (CTD)

练习 3

Sentence 1 作用：提出假设 (suggest)。

Sentence 2 作用：转折 (yet)，提出质疑和新的观点。

Sentence 3 作用：给出实例 (for example) 证明。

Sentence 4 作用：强调质疑的正确性。

Sentence 5 作用：得到结论 (if so)，提出警示 (wary)。

练习 4

Sentence 1 作用：给出很多人的观点。

Sentence 2 作用：转折，进行反驳。

Sentence 3 作用：给出一个原因。

Sentence 4 作用：对原因进行说明。

Sentences 5—6 作用：给出第二个原因。

Sentence 7 作用：第二个原因的另外一方面。

练习 5

Sentence 1 作用：提出其他人的观点。

Sentence 2 作用：观点的细节。

Sentence 3 作用：反驳以及分析后果。

SAT 官方试题例题分析——句子作用题

例 1

Humans vary across the world. Every independently conceived individual is genetically unique. This seems paradoxical in light of the fact that all humans have a high degree of genetic similarity. It is often reported that two humans are 99.9 percent similar in their DNA. However, the human genome is immense, providing multiple opportunities for genetic variation to arise, the 0.1 percent by which we differ amounts to 3. 3 million nucleotides. Findings from the International Hap MapMap Project confirm previous studies and show a relatively low amount of differentiation among human groups defined by ethnicity and geography. There is much more genetic variation within (about 90 percent) than among (about 10 percent) human groups. This means that the similarities among different groups of humans far outweigh the differences.

The information in lines 39–41 (“There…groups”) primarily serves to

A) provide more precise data regarding the degree of genetic overlap between members of different ethnic and geographic groups.

B) support the author’s claim that genetic profiling will enhance the ability to predict a group member’s predisposition to a particular disease.

C) further develop the idea that the human genome is much larger and more complicated than scientists originally thought.

D) call into question the results of the International HapMap Project and other studies regarding the diversity of the human genome.

【解析】Lines 39–41: There is much more genetic variation within (about 90 percent) than among (about 10 percent) human groups.

这句话从意思上非常好理解，主要是比较群体内部和群体之间的基因变化。而上一句表达的就是不同种族和地域的人群基因差异，所以这两句话题一致，而且没有转折或对比。

选项分析：

A 选项正确，因为表达的就是不同群体的基因重合度的准确数字 (90% 和 10%)。

B 选项错误，因为这句话及前后句没有提及预测群体得病倾向。

C 选项错误，因为本句并未表达人类基因的大小和复杂程度。

D 选项错误，因为并非质疑各类研究的结果。

像这道题其实只看这个句子即可，不看上下文也能找到正确答案。

例 2

However, political cyber-optimists have criticized cyber-pessimists for being too extreme and maintain that new media might be the decisive element in pushing the democratic agenda of elections nowadays. For instance, based on data published by the Pew Research Center, sixty-six percentage of social media users have participated in at least eight online political activities, such as encouraging people to vote or posting their comments on politics through social media. Thus, Internet voters may shape election campaign agendas to some extent. The fact that Barack Obama obtained an electoral victory following a triumphant grassroots campaign and successful use of social media such as Facebook and Myspace is a case in point.

The author uses the Pew Research Center findings to imply that

A) Barack Obama's victory was possible only because of social media usage.

B) new media users influence real-world political events to some degree.

C) cyber-optimists take an overly positive stance towards new media.

D) cyber-pessimists do not understand how new media outlets are used.

【解析】句 1 作用：提出乐观者的观点 (maintain) ——新媒体可能是推进民主进程的决定

性因素。

句 2 作用：举例 (for instance)——通过一个研究的结果论证前句观点。

句 3 作用：得到结论 (thus)。

句 4 作用：再举例 (a case in point)。

所以题目问 Pew Research Center finding, 也就是句 2 的作用，那么答案就是举例论证新媒体的使用可以推进民主进程。答案选择 B。这道题最好结合上下文对句子的作用进行判定，否则答案不一定能够选出来。

例 3

The health benefits of engaging in physical activity (PA) during childhood include enhanced fitness, cognitive function and bone health; reduced body fatness, motor skill development, and favourable cardiovascular and metabolic disease risk profiles. Being active during childhood can also improve self-esteem and reduce symptoms of anxiety and depression. Participation in PA in youth is of great importance as PA may track into adulthood where adequate levels of PA are protective against many chronic diseases. However, in the UK approximately 75% of boys and 80% of girls aged 5–10 years are not meeting the daily recommendation of 60 minutes of moderate to vigorous physical activity...

The statistics about UK children (lines 9–12) primarily serve to

A) encourage readers to become more active.

B) call attention to a particular situation.

C) transition to a discussion of unstructured and structured play.

D) introduce an argument that the authors will later contradict.

【解析】句 1 作用：描述参与体育运动 (physical activity) 的好处 (benefits)。

句 2 作用：继续 (also) 描述好处。

句 3 作用：得出观点 (importance)。

句 4 作用：转折 (however)，说明现状 (负面)。

所以本题答案选择 B 选项——关注一个特别的情况。特别的情况就是目前英国孩童参与运动的情况未能达标，情况令人担忧。

A 错误，因为没有鼓励读者。

C 错误，因为词句并未讨论 structured 或者 unstructured play。

D 错误，因为没有引出后文反驳的观点。此句是事实或现象，并非观点，而且后文并未反驳。

稍微作个总结，我们在做这类题时候，思考过程如下：

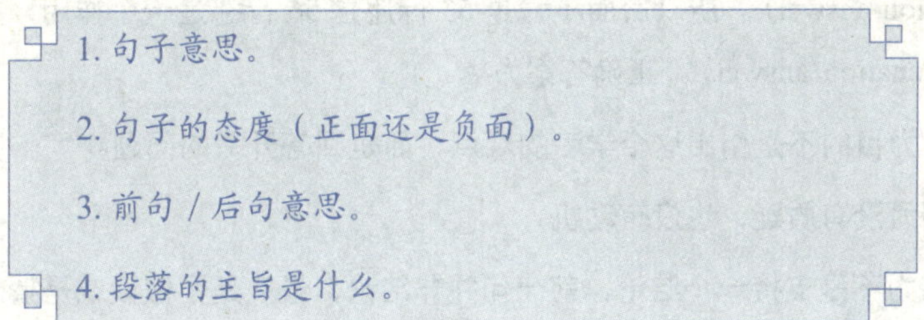

1. 句子意思。
2. 句子的态度（正面还是负面）。
3. 前句 / 后句意思。
4. 段落的主旨是什么。

通常，正确答案的描述就是围绕本句意思或者态度，或者整个段落主旨进行。大家在选择答案的时候可以判断选项的态度是否正确、话题是否正确、意思是否正确。

例 4

Why do gift-givers assume that gift price is closely linked to gift-recipients' feelings of appreciation? Perhaps givers believe that bigger (i.e, more expensive) gifts convey stronger signals of thoughtfulness and consideration. According to Camerer (1988) and others, gift-giving represents a symbolic ritual, whereby gift-givers attempt to signa their positive attitudes toward the intended recipient and their willingness to invest resources in a future relationship. In this sense, gift-givers may be motivated to spend more money on a gift in order to send a "stronger signa" to their intended recipient. As for gift-recipients, they may not construe smaller and larger gifts as representing smaller and larger signals of thoughtfulness and consideration.

The authors refer to work by Camerer and others (line 56) in order to

A) offer an explanation.

B) introduce an argument.

C) question a motive.

D) support a conclusion

【解析】这道题如果做错，大部分同学会选择 D 选项。因为如果只看 56 行那句话，会发现是一个学者的想法，在思考不充分的情况下会觉得这句话使用一个学者的观点来支持某个东西。

但是实际上，如果从整个段落的结构来看，这个段落首先是提出一个问题，后面很明显是提供答案（question-answer）。所以后面不管是 53 行还是 56 行都是一个作用：提供解释或答案（provide an explanation/answer）。正确答案为 A。

B 错误，因为目的不是引出这个学者的观点，而是回答开头的问题。

C 错误，因为没有质疑，也没有动机。

D 错误，因为不是支持一个结论，前一句并非结论，最多是个假设或是猜想。

SAT 官方试题例题分析——单词作用题

相比句子作用题，SAT 的试题中更倾向于考查某个单词的作用。题干的呈现方式有以下几种。

- In the passage, the reference to "..." mainly serves to...
- The author uses the word "..." in order to...
- The word "..." mainly serves to...
- The reference to "..." mainly has which effect?

在做这类单词 / 短语题的时候主要思考以下问题。

1. 单词是什么含义。
2. 单词表达什么态度或语气。
3. 单词所在句子的意思和作用。
4. 单词所在句子表达的态度和语气。

正确选项一般与这几个问题相关。下面我们选取一些官方试题进行分析。

例 1

The hydrogen proton can be likened to the planet earth, spinning on its axis, with a north-south pole. In this respect it behaves like a small bar magnet. Under normal circumstances, these hydrogen proton "bar magnets" spin in the body with their axes randomly aligned. When the body is placed in a strong magnetic field, such as an MRI scanner, the proton's axes all lined up. This uniform alignment creates a

The "planet earth" image in line 6 mainly serves to

A) highlight an unlikely parallel between the fields of biology and astronomy

B) inject a note of humor into an otherwise serious explanation of magnetic resonance imaging

C) create a pun centered on the idea that hydrogen is necessary for life on this planet

D) communicate a complex scientific idea using a more familiar concept

【解析】(1) 单词含义：planet earth“地球”，这个很简单，概念大家都熟悉。

(2) 单词没有语气或态度。

(3) 单词所在句子的意思：氢质子和地球很相似 (liken)，绕着轴旋转，都有南北极。作用：讲述氢质子的特点。

(4) 句子表达的态度或语气：句子采用比较轻松的语气在讲述科学信息，使用比喻的修辞手法。

A 选项错误，首先不是讲解生物学和天文学的概念，其次不是强调不可能的相似。

B 选项错误，这句话没有 humor，其次也不是讲解 MRI 的概念，而是讲解氢质子。

C 选项错误，单词或句子没有 pun“双关的修辞手法”。

D 选项正确，使用熟悉的概念 (地球) 表达复杂的含义 (氢质子的特点)。

例 2

Line

Willow trees are well-known sources of salicylic acid, and for thousands of years, humans have extracted the compound from the tree's bark to alleviate minor pain, fever, and inflammation.

Now, salicylic acid may also offer relief to crop plants by priming their defenses against a microbial menace known as "potato purple top phytoplasma." Outbreaks of the cell-wall-less bacterium in the fertile Columbia Basin region of the

The word "now" in line 5 mainly serves to

A) highlight the recent nature of a finding

B) inject a note of informality into a formal passage

C) suggest that humans no longer perform the activity mentioned in the first paragraph

D) create a sense of urgency in the passage

【解析】(1) 单词含义：now “现在”，时间概念。

(2) 单词没有语气或态度。

(3) 单词所在句子意思：现在，杨柳酸可以用来为植物提供治疗。

作用：说明杨柳酸的用处以及具体细节。

(4) 句子表达的态度或语气：和上段内容形成对比，强调杨柳酸新的用处。

A 正确，强调一项新的发现。

B 错误，now 这个单词和是否正式 (formal) 没有关系。

C 错误，没有提到人类不再做上段提及的活动。

D 错误，文章中的单词或句子没有体现紧迫感。

例 3

my darling, my cherished-in-secret, Imagination, the tender and the mighty, should never, either by softness or strength, have severed me. But this was not all; the antipathy which had sprung up between myself and my employer striking deeper root and spreading denser shade daily, excluded me from every glimpse of the sunshine of life; and I began to feel like a plant growing in humid darkness out of the slimy walls of a well.

The references to "shade" and "darkness" at the end of the first paragraph mainly have which effect?

A) They evoke the narrator's sense of dismay.

B) They reflect the narrator's sinister thoughts.

C) They capture the narrator's fear of confinement.

D) They reveal the narrator's longing for rest.

【解析】(1) 单词含义：shade "阴暗"，darkness "黑暗"。

(2) 单词态度或语气：负面态度。

(3) 单词所在句子意思：叙述者感觉自己像是生活在阴暗潮湿地方的植物，看不到阳光。

作用：用比如方式传达内心的情感——沮丧、失望和悲观。

(4) 句子表达的态度或语气：沮丧、失望和悲观。

A 正确，dismay "灰心；丧气"。

B 错误，没有邪恶的想法。

C 错误，没有害怕的情感。

D 错误，没有说渴望休息。

例 4

We've all heard the adage: practice makes perfect! In other words, acquiring skills takes time and effort. But how exactly does one go about learning a complex subject such as tennis, calculus, or how to play the violin? An age-old answer is: practice one skill at a time. A beginning pianist might rehearse scales before chords. A tennis player practices the forehand before the backhand. Learning researchers call this "blocking," and because it is commonsensical and easy to schedule, blocking is dominant in schools and training programs.

The main effect of the words "adage" in line 1 and "age-old" in line 4 is to

A) emphasize the prevalence of certain assumptions about learning

B) reveal that a method of learning has been extensively researched

C) highlight the reliability of a commonsense approach to learning

D) suggest that a style of learning is the subject of ongoing debate

【解析】(1) 单词含义：adage "格言"，age-old "古老的"。

(2) 单词态度或语气：偏正面（"格言" 说明被广为接受，"古老的" 说明流传已久）。

(3) 单词所在句子意思：大家都听过一句格言……有个古老的答案……。作用：表达大家对练习方法的普遍认知。

(4) 句子表达的态度或语气：无。

这道题大部分做错的同学会选择 C，但是正确答案为 A。这两个选项的主要差别在于 reliability 和 prevalence。题目问的是 "格言" 和 "古老的"，文章句子体现不出这种 "可靠性"，所以只能选择 "普遍性"。B 和 D 很明显是无中生有：B 项，原文没有提到被广泛研究，D 项，原文没有提到备受争议。

1. 真题练习

题 1

"Matter, sir? Oh, what could be the matter in your service. I've eaten your salt for all my years. But sir, on the bicycle now, with my old legs, and with the many injuries I've received when heavy machinery fell on me—I cannot any longer bicycle about like a bridegroom from farm to farm, as I could when I first had the good fortune to enter your employment, I beg you, sir, let me go."

Nawab uses the word "bridegroom" (line 62) mainly to emphasize that he's no longer

A) in love.

B) naive.

C) busy.

D) young.

题 2

When I so pressingly urge a strict observance of all the laws, let me not be understood as saying there are no bad laws, nor that grievances may not arise, for the redress of which, no legal provisions have been made. I mean to say no such thing. But I do mean to say, that, although bad laws, if they exist, should be repealed as soon as possible, still while they continue in force, for the sake of example, they should be religiously observed. So also in unprovided

The sentence in lines 24—28 ("When. made") primarily serves which function in Passage 1?

A) It raises and refutes a potential counterargument to Lincoln's argument.

B) It identifies and concedes a crucial shortcoming of Lincoln's argument.

C) It acknowledges and substantiates a centra assumption of lincoln's argument.

D) It anticipates and corrects a possible misinterpretation of lincoln's argument.

Even longer-term, Green is betting on silicon, aiming to take advantage of the huge reductions in cost already seen with the technology. He hopes to greatly increase the efficiency of silicon solar panels by combining silicon with one or two other semiconductors, each selected to efficiently convert a part of the solar spectrum that silicon doesn't convert efficiently. Adding one semiconductor could boost efficiencies from the 20 to 25 percent range to around 40 percent. Adding another could make efficiencies as high as 50 percent feasible, which would cut in half the number of solar panels needed for a given installation. The challenge is to produce good connections between these semiconductors, something made challenging by the arrangement of silicon atoms in crystalline silicon.

The last sentence of the passage mainly serves to

A) express concern about the limitations of a material.

B) identify a hurdle that must be overcome.

C) make a prediction about the effective use of certain devices.

D) introduce a potential new area of study.

Revolutions are sudden to the unthinking only. Strange rumblings and confused noises still precede these earthquakes and hurricanes of the moral world. The process of revolution in France has been dreadful, and should incite us to examine with an anxious eye the motives and manners of those, whose conduct and opinions seem calculated to forward a similar event in our own country. The oppositionists to "things as they arc" are divided into many and different classes. To delineate them with an unflattering accuracy may be a delicate, but it is a necessary, task, in order that we may enlighten, or at least be aware of, the misguided men who have enlisted under the banners of liberty, from no principles or with bad ones...

In the first paragraph, the author refers to "strange rumblings" and "confused noises" most likely to

A) suggest that there are always signs that a revolution will occur.

B) emphasize the chaos that typically accompanies revolution.

C) explain the unusual features of the French Revolution.

D) underscore the fear of many people about the possibility of revolution.

A long-term, large-scale study of a common weedy plant, *Plantago lanceolata*, and its fungal pathogen, powdery mildew conducted by Jussi Jousimo et al., involved a small army of about 40 field assistants who conducted annual censuses of 4000 populations over a 12-year period. The pattern revealed by this remarkable effort was surprising: The more connected a *Plantago* population was to other populations, the less likely it was to be colonized by the fungal pathogen.

The phrases “large-scale”and “small army,” used in the sentence in lines 11–16, mainly serve to emphasize the study’s

A) extensive scope.

B) paradoxical objectives.

C) unwieldy methods.

D) scientific importance.

The Bretton Woods system was hailed as a vast improvement over both ther rigid gold tandard of pre-1914 and the monetary anarchy of the interwar period. For a quarter-century, Bretton Woods undergirded a rare period of steady growth, full employment, and financial stability. But in many respects, the vaunted role of the World Bank, the International Monetary Fund, and the Bretton Wood rules specifying fixed exchange rates was a convenient mirage. The system’s true anchor was the United states—the U.S. dollar was de facto global currency: the U.S. economy as the residual consumer market for other nations' exports; and U.S. recovery aid in the form of the Marshall Plan, which dwarfed the outlays of the World Bank.

The author uses the phrase "convenient mirage" in line 73 mainly to

A) provide an example of the ways countries benefited from the convenience of the World Bank.

B) indicate that the ultimate success of Bretton Woods depended on the adoption of a Keynesian system.

C) illustrate the types of misleading tactics Britain and the United States used during diplomatic negotations.

D) enphasize that the achievements of the Bretton Woods system weren't as substantial as they seemed.

Writing to a colleague after the conference ended, Keynes professed to be pleased. He wrote that in the new International Monetary Fund, "we have in truth got both in substance and in phrasing all that we could reasonably hope for." The new World Bank, Keynes declared, offered "grand possibilities...The Americans are virtually pledging themselves to quite gigantic untied loans for reconstruction and development."

The quotations from Keynes in lines 32–38 ("we have...development") mainly serve to

A) illustrate keynes's expression of satifaction with the outcome of Bretton Woods.

B) articulate the agenda for monetary reform that Keynes presented at Bretton Woods.

C) support the author's claim that the new World Bank was crucial for postwar reconstruction.

D) argue that Keynes was more disappointed by the Bretton Woods system than he admitted.

This showed that the spotted green pigeon is indeed a separate species, showing a unique DNA barcode compared to other pigeons. The pigeon is genetically most closely related to the Nicobar pigeon and the dodo and Rodrigues solitaire, both extinct birds from islands near Madagascar.

The spotted green pigeon shows signs of a semi-terrestrial island lifestyle and the ability to fly. The closely related Nicobar pigeon shows similar habits and has a preference for travelling between small islands.

In Passage 2, the image of a barcode mainly serves to

A) trivialize the complexity of a particular research practice.

B) use a familiar concept to communicate an idea.

C) question the novelty of a scientific phenomenon.

D) inject a note of levity into an otherwise serious argument.

2. 答案与解析

题 1

答案选 D。

【解析】bridegroom 意思是“新郎”，再结合语境，“我”不能再骑自行车了，因为这两条腿老了，身体也受了一些伤，不能再像新郎一样骑车了。所以强调的是“身体虚弱，年龄增加”。

题 2

答案选 D。

【解析】这句话主要意思是：当我急切地呼吁大家去遵守法律的时候，不要误解我认为没有坏的法律，或者不会发生不公平的事情。所以，这句话主要是作者担心别人会曲解他的观点而作出的澄清说明。答案关键词为“误解 / 曲解”。

A 错误，并非别人对其的反对（counterargument）。

B 错误，并非承认自己观点的缺陷。

C 错误，并非证实自己观点的核心假设。

题 3

答案选 B。

【解析】最后一句话主句是“the challenge is to produce good connections”，主要说明面临什么挑战。关键词是“挑战”“难题”。

A 错误，并非材料的局限性，而是如何布局材料使得半导体之间产生很好的关联。

C 错误，并非预测任何东西。

D 错误，并非引出潜在研究领域。

题 4

答案选 A。

【解析】单词的意思是“奇怪的轰隆声”“混乱的噪音”。结合语境理解“Strange rumblings and confused noises still precede these earthquakes and hurricanes of the moral world.”，句子使用了暗喻的修辞手法，其中地震和暴风指的是第一句中的 revolutions（革命，变革）。而整个句子意思是在发生这些变革之前一定存在一些奇怪的和混乱的声音。再结合第一句“Revolutions are sudden to the unthinking only”，说明只有不思考的人才会觉得变革是突然的，因为在变革之前一定有征兆。

题 5

答案选 A。

【解析】根据这几个单词和文章的语境，主要是强调一个研究的范围。

题 6

答案选 D。

【解析】convenient mirage 的意思是“权宜的海市蜃楼”。海市蜃楼主要强调的是虚幻，不切实际。再结合语境，主要表达出世界银行、国际货币基金组织以及布雷顿森林体系的一些规则是海市蜃楼。所以选项 not as substantial as they seemed 正确。

题 7

答案选 A。

【解析】题目问凯恩斯说的话主要目的是什么。而通过引号中的用词和句子，可以很容易看出来是正面的态度，比如“got all that we could hope for”“grand possibilities”。所以这些话语表达出对会议的积极评价。A 选项正确。

题 8

答案选 B。

【解析】首先，很多同学可能不知道 barcode 的意思，认为无法选出正确答案。其实如果不认识这个单词，我们可以根据句子意思进行选择。整个句子意思是一个研究表明这种鸽子确实是一个单独的种类。说明这句话在表达一个从实验中得到的结论。

A 错误，并非减小实验的复杂性。因为这句话是实验结果，和实验的复杂性无关。

C 错误，并非质疑科学现象的新奇性。

D 错误，并非插入一种轻浮的语气。

所以答案选择 B，用一个大家熟悉的概念去传达观点。这也是科学类文章经常使用的方法，用生活中的例子或是各类修辞手法（比如拟人等）来表达有些晦涩的科学概念。

第六章

证据呢？询证题作答思路与步骤

询证题是新 SAT 设计的新题型，其重点在于考查学生得到上题答案或者本题题干某种观点 / 推测 / 结论的证据寻找的能力。

询证题是 SAT 中占比最多的题型，我们可以看一下有关官方指南上 8 套试题的统计。

官方试题（部分）	询证题数量	占比
SAT Practice Test 1	17	33%
SAT Practice Test 2	18	35%
SAT Practice Test 3	21	40%
SAT Practice Test 4	21	40%
SAT Practice Test 5	20	38%
SAT Practice Test 6	19	37%
SAT Practice Test 7	20	38%
SAT Practice Test 8	18	35%

可以看出，询证题在一套试题中占比高达 38% 甚至 40%。所以掌握询证题的做题方法和步骤对于提高 SAT 阅读分数有着至关重要的作用。

从出题的方式来看，询证题有如下三种。

第 *1* 种：文章单独询证题

比如：

Which choice best supports the author’s claim that there is common ground shared by the different approaches to ethics described in the passage?

A) Lines 11–12 (“There...decision”)

B) Lines 47–50 (“From...advertisements”)

C) Lines 59–64 (“Take...market”)

D) Lines 75–77 (“We...facts”)

这道题题干中直接给出考生需要找到的证据作用，需要能够支持 “author’s claim that there is common ground shared by the different approaches to ethics”。选项是文章中四个出处的句子。

再比如：

Which choice provides the best evidence that the author of Passage 2 would agree to some extent with the claim attributed to Michael Merzenich in lines 41–43, Passage 1?

A) Lines 51–53 (“Critics...brain”)

B) Lines 54–56 (“Yes...changes”)

C) Lines 57–59 (“But...experience”)

D) Lines 83–84 (“Media...consumes”)

这道题需要考生在第二篇中寻找作者在某种程度上同意 41—43 行 Michael 表达的观点。

第 2 种：文章双题询证题

比如：

上题

According to Peacock, the ability to monitor internal waves is significant primarily because

A) it will allow scientists to verify the maximum height of such waves.

B) it will allow researchers to shift their focus to improving the quality of satellite images.

C) the study of wave patterns will enable regions to predict and prevent coastal damage.

D) the study of such waves will inform the development of key scientific models.

下题

Which choice provides the best evidence for the answer to the previous question?

A) Lines 1–2 (“Some...see”)

B) Lines 4–6 (“they...equipment”)

C) Lines 17–19 (“If...this”)

D) Lines 24–26 (“Internal...high”)

这种题的特点是下题的题干出现 “previous question” 。所以需要考生找出得到上题答案的最佳证据。

第 3 种：图文结合询证题

在有图表的文章中，可能出现图表和文章关联的询证题，而不只是考查对文章的理解。

比如：

Which statement from the passage is most directly reflected by the data presented in the graph?

A) Lines 30–33 (“In their...interested”)

B) Lines 33–36 (“The unfortunate...scientist”)

C) Lines 43–45 (“Not unexpectedly...published”)

D) Lines 52–55 (“It’s a...Berkeley”)

这道题考查的是文章的哪个陈述是被图表所反映出来的。这类题首先需要识别图表的作用和信息，然后再去文章中找到对应的信息。

如何处理询证题

考试中最多的是双题询证题，所以我们主要分析这类题的做题思路和步骤。这类题有上下题两题，那么先做上题还是下题？还是两道题八个选项放在一起看呢？做题会不会费太多时间？其实掌握了正确的做题思路和步骤，大部分询证题是非常好处理的。

方法 *1*：先下题后上题

这种方法适用于上题是细节信息类的题目，也就是说，上题问的问题是关于文章中某句话的信息，而不是文章的主旨，也不是文章或一些人的态度。我们来举例说明。

比如上题题干：Which reaction does Akira most fear from Chie? 题干问的是 Akira 非常害怕 Chie 的什么反应。问题非常具体，应该是文章中某句话所提到的。关键词是 Akira、most fear、from Chie。所以我们可以先看下题选项。

A) Line 33 (“His voice...refined”)

“His voice was soft, refined.” 这句话并没有回答上题题干的问题。所以排除。

B) Lines 49–51 (“You...mind”)

“You know how children speak so earnestly, so hurriedly, so endearingly about things that have no importance in an adult’s mind?” 这句话是 Chie 对 Akira 的态度，但是没有说明是 Akira 所害怕的。

C) Lines 63–64 (“Please...proposal”)

“Please don’t judge my candidacy by the unseemliness of this proposal.” 这句话在文章中是 Akira 对 Chie 说的，通过 please don’t 这种表达说明 Akira 是害怕 / 担心 Chie 会质疑他的资格。所以回答了上题题干的问题，Akira 害怕的事情在这句话中体现出来了。

D) Lines 71–72 (“Eager...face”)

“Eager to make his point, he’d been looking her full in the face.” 和 A/B 选项一样，这句话也没有说明 Akira 害怕什么。故排除。

到这里，我们已经得到下题的答案，选择 C) Lines 63–64 (“Please...proposal”)。

然后我们根据 C 选项的行号内容进行理解：Akira 请求对方不要通过求婚的 unseemliness 去 judge 他的 candidacy。所以理解这几个关键词之后，上题答案就很容易选择出来；Akira 是请求 Chie 不要通过求婚的不合适来质疑他的资格。这个时候看上题选项。

A) She will consider his proposal inappropriate.

正确，inappropriate = unseemly，属于同义转述。

B) She will mistake his earnestness for immaturity.

错误，没有提到 immaturity。

C) She will consider his unscheduled visit an imposition.

错误，并不是担心 Chie 认为他的拜访是不请自来。

D) She will underestimate the sincerity of his emotions.

错误，并不是担心Chie低估他的真诚。

总结，用第一种方法做题包括这几个步骤：

1. 审题，上题题目问什么，关键词是什么？可以通过什么定位？

2. 看下题行号，哪个/哪些行号的内容和上题相关并回答上题问题？

3. 如果某个行号回答上题问题或是和上题相关，再看上题选项是否有同义转述。

4. 如果有，则是答案，如果不是同义转述，则排除。

方法2：先上题后下题

如果上题是主旨题/概括题/态度题，那么可以采用先上题后下题的方法。因为通常对于整篇文章或是某个段落的概括以及态度类的问题是不需要通过某几句话得出答案的，看完文章或是段落即可得出结论；这个时候可以直接把上题答案选出来，然后再根据上题的答案选出下题最好的证据。需要注意的是，下题的行号最好是完整对应上题答案的陈述。比如：

Of course, that's not how most environmentalists regard their arugula [a leafy green]. They have embraced organic food as better for the planet—and healthier and tastier, too—than the stuff produced by agricultural corporations. Environmentalists disdain the enormous amounts of energy needed and waste created by conventional farming, while organic practice—forgoing artificial fertilizers and chemical pesticides—are considered far more sustainable. Sales of organic food rose 7.7% in 2010, up to $26.7 billion—and people are making those purchases for their consciences as much as their taste buds.

Yet a new meta-analysis in *Nature* does the math and comes to a hard conclusion: organic farming yields 25% fewer crops on average than conventional agriculture. More land is therefore needed to produce fewer crops—and that means organic farming may not be as good for the planet as we think.

24

Which choice best reflects the perspective of the "environmentalists" (line 27) on conventional agriculture?

A) It produces inferior fruits and vegetables and is detrimental to the environment.

B) It is energy efficient and reduces the need to convert wilderness to farmland.

C) It is good for the environment only in the short run.

D) It depletes critical resources but protects wildlife habitats

25

Which choice provides the best evidence for the answer to the previous question?

A) Lines 27–28 (“Of course...green”)

B) Lines 28–31 (“They, corporations”)

C) Lines 31–35 (“Environmentalists...sustainable”)

D) Lines 42–45 (“More.think”)

【解析】首先上题 24 题是一道态度题，问的是环保主义者对于传统农业的态度。从文章段落中明显可以看到态度是负面的。所以 24 题答案可以排除所有带有正面选项的单词。

A 正确，inferior、detrimental 这两个形容词都是负面的。

B 错误，energy efficient 是正面的，不是环保主义者的态度。

C 错误，没有提到短期对环境有好处。

D 错误，protect wildlife 正面，文章未提及。

第 24 题得到 A 答案之后，如何选择第 25 题的证据呢？（大部分同学认为应该选 C）

这个时候我们需要根据上题的答案陈述来找下题行号——it produces inferior fruits and vegetables and is detrimental to the environment，这里提到了两点：一是传统农业生产的水果和蔬菜质量差；二是对环境有害。

而 C 选项只提到了对环境的影响，没有提到 inferior fruits and vegetables，所以不够全面；而 B 选项中提到 organic food 是 better for the planet，以及 healthier and tastier too，两个点都能对应。所以最好的证据 (best evidence) 是 B。

有同学会有疑问，题目不是问环保主义者对传统农业的态度么？证据中的 B 选项说的是 organic food（有机食品）啊。但是，需要注意这个段落是对比结构，可以推理出环保主义者认为传统农业生产的食品不够健康和美味并且对地球有害。B 是最全面的（C 并没有错，只是没有 B 好；因为题目问的是 best evidence）。

总结，用方法 2 作答包括这几个步骤：

1. 判断上题为主旨题 / 概括题 / 态度题，可以直接根据对文章的理解选择答案。

2. 再次看一下对上题选项的描述，有哪些关键词。

3. 根据上题选项找出意思最接近而且表达最全面的证据行号。

总体来说，就是非常简单的两个步骤。

步骤 *1*：题干问题是什么？

步骤 *2*：哪些行号在回答问题？

对于图文结合的询证题，需要先了解图表的作用和细节，根据题目要求去寻找证据。

文章双题询证题

练习 1

Questions 43–52 are based on the following passage and supplementary material.

This passage is adapted from Geoffrey Giller, "Long a Mystery, How 500-Meter-High Undersea Waves Form Is Revealed." ©2014 by *Scientific American*.

Some of the largest ocean waves in the world are nearly impossible to see. Unlike other large waves, these rollers, called internal waves, do not ride the ocean surface. Instead, they move underwater, undetectable without the use of satellite imagery or sophisticated monitoring equipment. Despite their hidden nature, internal waves are fundamental parts of ocean water dynamics, transferring heat to the ocean depths and bringing up cold water from below. And they can reach staggering heights—some as tall as skyscrapers.

Because these waves are involved in ocean mixing and thus the transfer of heat, understanding them is crucial to global climate modeling, says Tom Peacock, a researcher at the Massachusetts Institute of Technology. Most models fail to take internal waves into account. "If we want to have more and more accurate climate models, we have to be able to capture processes such as this," Peacock says.

Peacock and his colleagues tried to do just that. Their study, published in November in *Geophysical Research Letters*, focused on internal waves generated in the Luzon Strait, which separates Taiwan and the Philippines. Internal waves in this region, thought to be some of the largest in the world, can reach about

500 meters high. "That's the same height as the Freedom Tower that's just been built in New York," Peacock says.

Although scientists knew of this phenomenon in the South China Sea and beyond, they didn't know exactly how internal waves formed. To find out, Peacock and a team of researchers from M.I.T. and Woods Hole Oceanographic Institution worked with France's National Center for Scientific Research using a giant facility there called the Coriolis Platform. The rotating platform, about 15 meters (49.2 feet) in diameter, turns at variable speeds and can simulate Earth's rotation. It also has walls, which means scientists can fill it with water and create accurate, large-scale simulations of various oceanographic scenarios.

Peacock and his team built a carbon-fiber resin scale model of the Luzon Strait, including the islands and surrounding ocean floor topography. Then they filled the platform with water of varying salinity to replicate the different densities found at the strait, with denser, saltier water below and lighter, less briny water above. Small particles were added to the solution and illuminated with lights from below in order to track how the liquid moved. Finally, they re-created tides using two large plungers to see how the internal waves themselves formed.

The Luzon Strait's underwater topography, with a distinct double-ridge shape, turns out to be responsible for generating the underwater waves. As the tide rises and falls and water moves through the strait, colder, denser water is pushed up over the ridges into warmer, less dense layers above it. This action results in bumps of colder water trailed by warmer water that generate an internal wave. As these waves move toward land, they become steeper—much the same way waves at the beach become taller before they hit the shore—until they break on a continental shelf.

The researchers were also able to devise a mathematical model that describes the movement and formation of these waves. Whereas the model is specific to the Luzon Strait, it can still help researchers understand how internal waves are generated in other places around the world. Eventually, this information will be incorporated into global climate models, making them more accurate. "It's very clear, within the context of these [global climate] models, that internal waves play a role in driving ocean circulations," Peacock says.

题 1

According to Peacock, the ability to monitor internal waves is significant primarily because

A) it will allow scientists to verify the maximum height of such waves.

B) it will allow researchers to shift their focus to improving the quality of satellite images.

C) the study of wave patterns will enable regions to predict and prevent coastal damage.

D) the study of such waves will inform the development of key scientific models.

题 2

Which choice provides the best evidence for the answer to the previous question?

A) Lines 1–2 ("Some...see")

B) Lines 4–6 ("they...equipment")

C) Lines 17–19 ("If...this")

D) Lines 24–26 ("Internal...high")

题 3

Based on information in the passage, it can reasonably be inferred that all internal waves

A) reach approximately the same height even though the locations and depths of continental shelves vary.

B) may be caused by similar factors but are influenced by the distinct topographies of different regions.

C) can be traced to inconsistencies in the tidal patterns of deep ocean water located near islands.

D) are generated by the movement of dense water over a relatively flat section of the ocean floor.

题 4

Which choice provides the best evidence for the answer to the previous question?

A) Lines 29–31 ("Although...formed")

B) Lines 56–58 ("As the...it")

C) Lines 61–64 ("As these...shelf")

D) Lines 67–70 ("Whereas...world")

练习 2

Questions 43–52 are based on the following passage and supplementary material.

This passage is adapted from Kevin Bullis, "What Tech Is Next for the Solar Industry?" ©2013 by *MIT Technology Review.*

Solar panel installations continue to grow quickly, but the solar panel manufacturing industry is in the doldrums because supply far exceeds demand. The poor market may be slowing innovation, but advances continue; judging by the mood this week at the IEEE Photovoltaics Specialists Conference in Tampa, Florida, people in the industry remain optimistic about its long-term prospects.

The technology that's surprised almost everyone is conventional crystalline silicon. A few years ago, silicon solar panels cost $4 per watt, and Martin Green, professor at the University of New South Wales and one of the leading silicon solar panel researchers, declared that they'd never go below $1 a watt. "Now it's down to something like 50 cents a watt, and there's talk of hitting 36 cents per watt," he says.

The U.S. Department of Energy has set a goal of reaching less than $1 a watt—not just for the solar panels, but for complete, installed systems—by 2020. Green thinks the solar industry will hit that target even sooner than that. If so, that would bring the direct cost of solar power to six cents per kilowatt-hour, which is cheaper than the average cost expected for power from new natural gas power plants.

All parts of the silicon solar panel industry have been looking for ways to cut costs and improve the power output of solar panels, and that's led to steady cost reductions. Green points to something as mundane as the pastes used to screen-print some of the features on solar panels. Green's lab built a solar cell in the 1990s that set a record efficiency for silicon solar cells—a record that stands to this day. To achieve that record, he had to use expensive lithography techniques to make fine wires for collecting current from the solar cell. But gradual improvements have made it possible to use screen printing to produce ever-finer lines. Recent research suggests that screen-printing techniques can produce lines as thin as 30 micrometers—about the width of the lines Green used for his record solar cells, but at costs far lower than his lithography techniques.

Meanwhile, researchers at the National Renewable Energy Laboratory have made flexible solar cells on a new type of glass from Corning called Willow Glass, which is thin and can be rolled up. The type of solar cell they made is the only current challenger to silicon in terms of large-scale production—thin-film cadmium telluride. Flexible solar cells could lower the cost of installing solar cells, making solar power cheaper.

One of Green's former students and colleagues, Jianhua Zhao, cofounder of solar panel manufacturer China Sunergy, announced this week that he is building a pilot manufacturing line for a two-sided solar cell that can absorb light from both the front and back. The basic idea, which isn't new, is that during some parts of the day, sunlight falls on the land between rows of solar panels in a solar power plant. That light reflects onto the back of the panels and could be harvested to increase the power output. This works particularly well when the solar panels are built on sand, which is highly reflective. Where a one-sided solar panel might generate 340 watts, a two-sided one might generate up to 400 watts. He expects the panels to generate 10 to 20 percent more electricity over the course of a year.

Even longer-term, Green is betting on silicon, aiming to take advantage of the huge reductions in cost already seen with the technology. He hopes to greatly increase the efficiency of silicon solar panels by combining silicon with one or two other semiconductors, each selected to efficiently convert a part of the solar spectrum that silicon doesn't convert efficiently. Adding one semiconductor could boost efficiencies from the 20 to 25 percent range to around 40 percent. Adding another could make efficiencies as high as 50 percent feasible, which would cut in half the number of solar panels needed for a given installation. The challenge is to produce good connections between these semiconductors, something made challenging by the arrangement of silicon atoms in crystalline silicon.

题 1

It can most reasonably be inferred from the passage that many people in the solar panel industry believe that

A) consumers don't understand how solar panels work.

B) two-sided cells have weaknesses that have not yet been discovered.

C) the cost of solar panels is too high and their power output too low.

D) Willow Glass is too inefficient to be marketable.

题 2

Which choice provides the best evidence for the answer to the previous question?

A) Lines 1–3 ("Solar...demand")

B) Lines 10–15 ("A few...a watt")

C) Lines 22–26 ("If so...plants")

D) Lines 27–30 ("All...reductions")

 3

According to the passage, two-sided solar panels will likely raise efficiency by

A) requiring little energy to operate.

B) absorbing reflected light.

C) being reasonably inexpensive to manufacture.

D) preventing light from reaching the ground.

 4

Which choice provides the best evidence for the answer to the previous question?

A) Lines 58–61 ("The basic...plant")

B) Lines 61–62 ("That...output")

C) Lines 63–64 ("This...reflective")

D) Lines 64–66 ("Where...400 watts")

练习 3

This passage is adapted from Madhuvanthi Kannan, "Overworking Your Brain Can Spark Ideas." ©2015 by *Scientific American*.

If you walk down to the office gallery at Pearlfisher Inc., a design agency, you are bound to hear the unmistakable cluck of plastic balls colliding. At first, you might dismiss it as the sound of employees chilling out on a ping pong game. What you see next might take your breath away—a huge ball pit filled with 81,000 white plastic balls. But frolicking in the pit are not preschoolers or kindergartners. They are in fact corporate managers, dressed in business suits, in an afternoon brainstorming session.

Companies relying on innovation go to astonishing lengths to imbue creativity in their staff. Jump In!, the wacky brainchild of Pearlfisher's creative strategist, is built on the premise that interleaving work and play can spark creativity in grown-ups, just like it did back in school days.

But it turns out that mental exhaustion from overwork can itself unleash creativity. When we are tired, our mind can be too weary to control our thoughts, and eccentric ideas that might normally be filtered out can bubble up, suggests a recent study by RémiRadel at the University of Nice. This means that perhaps creative ideas can be hatched at the workplace, right when we feel drained from a mental overload.

In their study, Radel and colleagues overtaxed the minds of a group of undergrads by having them perform a computerized task that demanded attention: finding the direction of a center arrow by ignoring the directions of surrounding arrows. The task was iterated across 2000 trials. In conflict trials, the center and surrounding arrows pointed in opposite directions whereas in non-conflict trials, all arrows pointed in the same direction. The controls and test subjects faced conflict in 10% and 50% of the trials, respectively. After the students finished the task, the scientists measured their creativity in verbal tests. First, they asked the students to enlist multiple, innovative uses for common objects, such as paperclip, newspaper, shoe. Next, they tested the students' ability to connect unrelated words. They presented the students with a "priming word" followed by "target word"—for example, they flashed the word tiger followed by the word loni, jumbled from lion—and asked the students to vote whether the target word was a real or a non-existent word.

Radel found that students who took the rigorous attention task turned out to be more creative than others who had taken milder versions of the task. These students were also more likely to connect unrelated words in the word association test. They identified more non-existent words as real words especially when the prime-target pairs were seemingly related, such as tiger and loni. They perceived loni as lion when it appeared after tiger and hence, called it a real word. Their ability to associate unrelated words came from a reduced filtering of irrelevant information—here, for instance, the priming word tiger—from the mind.

Radel's attention task induced creativity in the students by exhausting their inhibition, which is the brain's ability to sift out unwanted information from the conscious mind. Although inhibition is essential for day-to-day activities such as problem solving and focusing on tasks, it stifles creative thinking by gating out eccentric thoughts and ideas. Being creative is not just about achieving a state of low inhibition, but about tweaking inhibition for brief stints without losing control. Harvard psychologist Shelly Carson calls this process "flexing the brain." She says that creative people can turn down the volume of inhibition to let novel ideas inspire them, and then, turn the volume back up to put their ideas to meaningful use.

For beginners, Radel's technique of overtaxing the brain, to find a sweet window for a creative spell, may be a good place to start. As we go through our day, juggling multiple tasks, our mind works hard to stay focused on a single task. There is the added pressure to keep distractions at bay—meetings, e-mails, news updates. At the end of it all, we are left feeling exhausted. At such times, instead of shutting down and relaxing, we should perhaps learn to capitalize on the mental fatigue and try to kindle our creative genius.

题 1

The passage suggests that one reason subjects in the control group connected fewer unrelated words on average than did subjects in the experimental group is that the subjects in the control group were more likely to

A) become distracted due to mental exhaustion.

B) demonstrate their creativity in unexpected ways.

C) exclude the priming words from conscious thought.

D) mistake the jumbled words for real words.

题 2

Which choice provides the best evidence for the answer to the previous question?

A) Lines 35–39 ("They presented...word")

B) Lines 42–43 ("These...test")

C) Lines 46–47 ("They perceived...word")

D) Lines 47–50 ("Their...mind")

题 3

It can most reasonably be inferred that the author regards mental exhaustion as

A) a potential opportunity for creative inspiration that should be pursued.

B) an unpleasant consequence that results from performing mundane activities.

C) a state that is less inclined to artistic invention than a state of mental alertness.

D) the ideal condition in which to focus on multiple tasks.

题 4

Which choice provides the best evidence for the answer to the previous question?

A) Lines 11–14 (“Jump...days”)

B) Lines 16–19 (“When...Nice”)

C) Lines 65–68 (“As...updates”)

D) Lines 69–71 (“At such...genius”)

练习 4

This passage is adapted from Steven C. Pan, “The Interleaving Effect: Mixing It up Boosts Learning.” © 2015 by *Scientific American*.

We’ve all heard the adage: practice makes perfect! In other words, acquiring skills takes time and effort. But how exactly does one go about learning a complex subject such as tennis, calculus, or how to play the violin? An age-old answer is: practice one skill at a time. A beginning pianist might rehearse scales before chords. A tennis player practices the forehand before the backhand. Learning researchers call this “blocking, ” and because it is commonsensical and easy to schedule, blocking is dominant in schools and training programs, and other settings.

However, another strategy promises improved results. Enter “interleaving,” a largely unheard-of technique that is capturing the attention of cognitive psychologists and neuroscientists. Whereas blocking involves practicing one skill at a time before the next (for example, “skill A” before —skill B and so on, forming the pattern “AAABBBCCC”), in interleaving one mixes, or interleaves, practice on several related skills together (forming for example the pattern “ABCABCABC”). For instance, a pianist alternates practice between scales, chords, and arpeggios, while a tennis player alternates practice between forehands, backhands, and volleys.

Given interleaving’s promise, it is surprising then that few studies have investigated its utility in everyday applications. However, a new study by cognitive psychologist Doug Rohrer takes a step towards addressing that gap. Rohrer and his team are the first to implement interleaving in actual classrooms. The location: middle schools in Tampa, Florida.

The target skills: algebra and geometry.

The three-month study involved teaching 7th graders slope and graph problems. Weekly lessons were largely unchanged from standard practice. Weekly homework worksheets, however, featured an interleaved or blocked design. When interleaved, both old and new problems of different types were mixed together. Of the nine participating classes, five used interleaving for slope problems and blocking for graph problems; the reverse occurred in the remaining four. Five days after the last lesson, each class held a review session for all students. A surprise final test occurred one day or one month later. The result? When the test was one day later, scores were 25 percent better for problems trained with interleaving; at one month later, the interleaving advantage grew to 76 percent.

These results are important for a host of reasons. First, they show that interleaving works in real-world, extended use. It is highly effective with an almost ubiquitous subject, math. The interleaving effect is long-term and the advantage over blocking actually increases with the passage of time. The benefit even persists when blocked materials receive additional review. Overall, the interleaving effect can be strong, stable, and long-lasting.

Researchers are now working to understand why interleaving yields such impressive results. One prominent explanation is that it improves the brain's ability to tell apart concepts. With blocking, once you know what solution to use, the hard part is over. With interleaving, each practice attempt is different from the last, so rote responses don't work. Instead, your brain must continuously focus on searching for different solutions. That process can improve your ability to learn critical features of skills.

A second explanation is that interleaving strengthens memory associations. With blocking, a single strategy, temporarily held in short-term memory, is sufficient. That's not the case with interleaving—the correct solution changes from one practice attempt to the next. As a result, your brain is continually engaged at retrieving different responses and bringing them into short-term memory.

Both of these accounts imply that increased effort during training is needed when interleaving is used. This corresponds to a potential drawback of the technique, namely that the learning process often feels more gradual and difficult at the outset. However, that added effort can generate better, longer-lasting results.

题 1

It can reasonably be inferred from the passage that most researchers interested in skills acquisition are

A) unconcerned with the relevance of interleaving to people's routine activities.

B) focused on how interleaving improves athletes' performance.

C) intent on examining the function of blocking within an educational setting.

D) undecided about whether interleaving is an effective alternative to blocking

题 2

Which choice provides the best evidence for the answer to the previous question?

A) Lines 7–10 ("Learning...programs")

B) Lines 14–19 ("Whereas...ABCABCABC")

C) Lines 19–22 ("For...volleys")

D) Lines 23–24 ("Given...applications")

题 3

The author of the passage would most likely agree with which perspective on interleaving?

A) It is more beneficial when an individual wants to learn numerous unrelated skills than when an individual wants to learn several related skills.

B) It may demand more time and exertion than other approaches to learning but is likely to have a more valuable outcome.

C) If it is applied consistently, it can train the brain to distinguish between relevant and irrelevant information.

D) It may require more studies on its effectiveness before neuroscientists recommend it be used in classroom instruction.

题 4

Which choice provides the best evidence for the answer to the previous question?

A) Lines 48–50 ("The benefit...review")

B) Lines 53–56 ("One...over")

C) Lines 62–65 ("With...next")

D) Lines 69–73 ("This...results")

文章单独询证题

练习 1

Time is probably no more unkind to sporting characters than it is to other people, but physical decay unsustained by respectability is somehow more noticeable. Mr. Peters' hair was turning gray and his scalp showed through on top. He had lost weight also; he no longer filled out his clothes the way he used to. His color was poor, and the flower had disappeared from his buttonhole. In its place was an American Legion button.

Apparently he himself was not aware that there had been any change. He straightened his tie self-consciously and when Irma handed him a menu, he gestured with it so that the two women at the next table would notice the diamond ring on the fourth finger of his right hand. Both of these things, and also the fact that his hands showed signs of the manicurist, one can blame on the young man who had his picture taken with a derby hat on the back of his head, and also sitting with a girl in the curve of the moon. The young man had never for one second deserted Mr. Peters. He was always there, tugging at Mr. Peters' elbow, making him do things that were not becoming in a man of forty-five.

Which choice best supports the conclusion that Mr. Peters wants to attract attention?

A) Lines 80–81 ("Apparently...change")

B) Lines 81–85 ("He straightened...hand")

C) Lines 90–91 ("The young...Mr. Peters")

D) Lines 91–93 ("He was...forty-five")

练习 2

Questions 32–41 are based on the following passage and supplementary material.

This passage is adapted from John Bohannon, "Why You Shouldn't Trust Internet Comments." ©2013 by *American Association for the Advancement of Science.*

The "wisdom of crowds" has become a mantra of the Internet age. Need to choose a new vacuum cleaner? Check out the reviews on online merchant Amazon. But a new study suggests that such online scores don't always reveal the best choice. A massive controlled experiment of Web users finds that such ratings are highly susceptible to irrational "herd behavior"—and that the herd can be manipulated.

Sometimes the crowd really is wiser than you. The classic examples are guessing the weight of a bull or the number of gumballs in a jar. Your guess is probably going to be far from the mark, whereas the average of many people's choices is remarkably close to the true number.

But what happens when the goal is to judge something less tangible, such as the quality or worth of a product? According to one theory, the wisdom of the crowd still holds—measuring the aggregate of people's opinions produces a stable, reliable value. Skeptics, however, argue that people's opinions are easily swayed by those of others. So nudging a crowd early on by presenting contrary opinions—for example, exposing them to some very good or very bad attitudes—will steer the crowd in a different direction. To test which hypothesis is true, you would need to manipulate huge numbers of people, exposing them to false information and determining how it affects their opinions.

A team led by Sinan Aral, a network scientist at the Massachusetts Institute of Technology in Cambridge, did exactly that. Aral has been secretly working with a popular website that aggregates news stories. The website allows users to make comments about news stories and vote each other's comments up or down. The vote tallies are visible as a number next to each comment, and the position of the comments is chronological. (Stories on the site get an average of about ten comments and about three votes per comment.) It's a follow-up to his experiment using people's ratings of movies to measure how much individual people influence each other online (answer: a lot). This time, he wanted to know how much the crowd influences the individual, and whether it can be controlled from outside.

For five months, every comment submitted by a user randomly received an "up" vote (positive); a "down" vote (negative); or as a control, no vote at all. The team then observed how users rated those comments. The users generated more than 100,000 comments that were viewed more than 10 million times and rated more than 300,000 times by other users.

At least when it comes to comments on news sites, the crowd is more herdlike than wise. Comments that received fake positive votes from the researchers were 32% more likely to receive more positive votes compared with a control, the team reports. And those comments were no more likely than the control to be down-voted by the next viewer to see them. By the end of the study, positively manipulated comments got an overall boost of about 25%. However, the same did not hold true for negative manipulation. The ratings of comments that got a fake down vote were usually negated by an up vote by the next user to see them.

"Our experiment does not reveal the psychology behind people's decisions," Aral says, "but an intuitive explanation is that people are more skeptical of negative social influence. They're more willing to go along with positive opinions from other people."

Duncan Watts, a network scientist at Microsoft Research in New York City, agrees with that conclusion. "[But] one question is whether the positive [herding] bias is specific to this site" or true in general, Watts says. He points out that the category of the news items in the experiment had a strong effect on how much people could be manipulated. "I would have thought that 'business' is pretty similar to 'economics,' yet they find a much stronger effect (almost 50% stronger) for the former than the latter. What explains this difference? If we're going to apply these findings in the real world, we'll need to know the answers."

Will companies be able to boost their products by manipulating online ratings on a massive scale? "That is easier said than done," Watts says. If people detect—or learn—that comments on a website are being manipulated, the herd may spook and leave entirely.

Which choice best supports the view of the "skeptics" (line 20)?

A) Lines 55–58 ("Comments...reports")

B) Lines 58–60 ("And...them")

C) Lines 63–65 ("The ratings...them")

D) Lines 76–79 ("He...manipulated")

练习 3

Questions 11–21 are based on the following passage and supplementary material.

This passage is adapted from Nicholas Epley, *Mindwise: How We Understand What Others Think, Believe, Feel, and Want*. ©2014 by Nicholas Epley.

Knowing your own reputation can be surprisingly difficult. Consider, for instance, a study that analyzed a set of published experiments all sharing the same basic design. In these experiments, people working in a group would be asked to predict how the other group members would rate them on a series of different traits. Researchers then compared these predicted ratings to the other group members' actual ratings on the very same traits. The traits varied from one experiment to another and included qualities like intelligence, sense of humor, consideration, defensiveness, friendliness, and leadership ability. The groups varied in familiarity, with the members of some groups being fairly unfamiliar with one another (such as having met only once, in a job interview) and the members of other groups being very familiar with one another (such as having lived together for an extended time as roommates). If people knew exactly what others were thinking, then there would be a perfect correspondence between predicted and actual ratings. If people were clueless, then there would be no correspondence between the two. Statistically speaking, you measure relationships like these with a correlation, where perfect correspondence yields a correlation of 1 and no correspondence yields a correlation of 0. The closer the correlation is to 1, the stronger the relationship.

First, the good news. These experiments suggested that people are pretty good, overall, at guessing how a group of others would evaluate them, on average. The overall correlation in these experiments between predicted impressions and the average actual impression of the group was quite high (.55, if you are quantitatively inclined). To put that in perspective, this is roughly the same magnitude as the correlation between the heights of fathers and the heights of sons (around .5). It is not perfect insight, but it is also very far from being clueless. In other words, you probably have a decent sense of what others generally think of you, on average.

Now the bad news. These experiments also assessed how well people could predict the impression of any single individual within a given group. You may know, for instance, that your coworkers in general think you are rather smart, but those coworkers also vary in their impression of you. Some think you are as sharp as a knife. Others think you are as sharp as a spoon. Do you know the difference?

Evidently, no. The accuracy rate across these experiments was barely better than random guessing (an overall correlation of .13 between predicted and actual evaluations, only slightly higher than no relationship whatsoever). Although you might have some sense of how smart your coworkers think you are, you appear to have no clue about which coworkers in particular find you smart and which do not. As one author of the study writes, "People seem to have just a tiny glimmer of insight into how they are uniquely viewed by particular other people."

But perhaps this is holding your mind-reading abilities to too high a standard? It's hard, after all, to define traits like intelligence and trustworthiness precisely, so it might not be so surprising that we have difficulty guessing how others will evaluate us on these ambiguous traits. What about predicting something simpler, such as how much other people like you? Surely you are better at this. You learn over time to hang around people who smile at you and avoid those who spit at you. You must have a much better sense of who likes you and who hates you within a group. Yes?

I'm afraid not. These studies found that people are only slightly better than chance at guessing who in a group likes them and who does not (the average correlation here was a meager .18). Some of your coworkers like you and others do not, but I wouldn't count on you knowing the difference. The same barely-better-than-guessing accuracy is also found in experiments investigating how well speed daters can assess who wants to date them and who does not, how well job candidates can judge which interviewers were impressed by them and which were not, and even how well teachers can predict their course evaluations. Granted, it's rare that you are completely clueless about how you are evaluated. Accuracy tends to be better than chance in these experiments, but not necessarily by very much.

Which choice best supports the claim in the first sentence of the passage?

A) Lines 2–4 ("Consider...design")

B) Lines 21–23 ("If people...two")

C) Lines 26–27 ("The closer...relationship")

D) Lines 54–58 ("Although...not")

答案与解析

一、文章双题询证题

练习 1

题 1

答案选 D。

题 2

答案选 C。

题 3

答案选 B。

题 4

答案选 D。

【解析】(题 1—2)：

第 1 题题干很具体(According to Peacock, the ability to monitor internal waves is significant primarily because)，有很多关键词，比如 Peacock、the ability to monitor internal waves，题目问的是这种能力很重要的原因是什么。

所以我们采用方法 1(先下题后上题进行处理)。先看下题的行号，哪句话是 Peacock 的观点，而且是 monitor internal waves 的原因和意义。

A 只是说有些 waves 是看不见的，和上题题干没有关系。

B 只是讲 internal waves 很难被发现，和 Peacock 或者 monitor 的意义无关。

C 引号中是 Peacock 说的话，所以和上题题干有关；另外内容说的是“如果我们想获得更加准确的天气模型，就必须要记录这种过程”。而 processes such as this (这种过程) 就是指代 to monitor internal waves，所以又和上题题干相关。

D 说的是某个地方 internal waves 的高度，和上题题干无关。

然后根据证据题的答案 C 的行号理解原文，再去选择上题答案，意义在于获得更准确的天气模型；所以第 1 题选 D (key scientific models)。

(题 3—4)：

第三题题干的关键词为“all internal waves”，其中很重要的一个词为“all”，整篇文章的话题是 internal waves，所以如果根据 internal waves 去思考，那么文章每个地方都可能是答案。但是因为加上 all 这个词，说明下面的证据应该讲的是“所有的”internal waves。按照这个思路我们去看第 4 题的证据行号。

A: “Although scientists knew of this phenomenon in the South China Sea and beyond, they didn’t know exactly how internal waves formed.” 这里面出现了 internal waves，而且是泛指，所以可能是上题答案，然后理解一下这句话意思“科学家不知道是怎么形成的”。回去看第 3 题选项，结果没有与此对应的答案，故排除。

B: “As the tide rises and falls and water moves through the strait, colder, denser water is pushed up over the ridges into warmer, less dense layers above it.” 首先这句话不能说明所有的 internal waves 怎么样，所以直接排除 (因为这个段落整体讲的是 Luzon Strait 这个海峡的波浪细节)。

C: 同理可以排除，并不能回答 all internal waves 怎么样。

D: “Whereas the model is specific to the Luzon Strait, it can still help researchers understand how internal waves are generated in other places around the world.” 这里出现了 internal waves，而且是 other places around the world，所以回答了所有的 internal waves 怎么样。然后再看这句话的具体内容：虽然这个模型是特定于 Luzon 海峡，但是它可以帮助科学家了解其他所有地方的波浪的形成。言外之意就是每个地方的 internal waves 都很特别，但也有相似之处 (不然通过一个模型也无法了解所有的 internal waves)。根据这个选项意思可以得到第 3 题答案为 B。

练习 2

题 1

答案选 C。

题 2

答案选 D。

题 3

答案选 B。

题 4

答案选 B。

【解析】(题 1—2)：

第一题题干的关键词为 many people in the...industry 和 believe，也就是说，题目问的是这个行业内很多人的想法是什么。所以我们可以直接从第二题入手，看看哪句话是行业内很多人的想法。

A 选项："Solar panel installations continue to grow quickly, but the solar panel manufacturing industry is in the doldrums because supply far exceeds demand." 所述内容和行业内很多人的想法无关，排除。

B 选项："A few years ago, silicon solar panels cost $4 per watt, and Martin Green, professor at the University of New South Wales and one of the leading silicon solar panel researchers, declared that they'd never go below $1 a watt." 虽然提到了行业内的个别学者，但是不能代表很多人(many people)，排除。

C 选项："If so, that would bring the direct cost of solar power to six cents per kilowatt-hour, which is cheaper than the average cost expected for power from new natural gas powerplants." 这句话是一个假设性场景，而且从前一句可以知道其实还只是 Green 的推测，也不能代表很多人的想法，排除。

D 选项："All parts of the silicon solar panel industry have been looking for ways to cut costs and improve the power output of solar panels, and that's led to steady cost reductions." 很明显，通过 all parts of the industry 可以看出来和上题题干关键词对应，所以可以判定是正确答案。

根据 D 选项行号描述，行业内各个方面都寻求方法来降低成本和提升输出，再去选择第一题答案。第一题很容易选择 C "他们认为成本太高以及输出太低"，所以才会想方法去改进提高。

(题 3—4)：

第三题题干关键词非常具体，所以还是采用先看下题行号再寻找上题答案的方法。上题关键词为 two-sided solar panels 以及 raise efficiency，问题问通过什么方式提高效率。

所以先看证据，很明显，B 选项 "That light reflects onto the back of the panels and could be harvested to increase the power output" 正确。因为这句话有关键词是在讨论 two-sided solar panels 那个段落，而且提到了如何增加 power output，对应上题题干中的 raise efficiency。再根据这句话的意思选择上题答案 B。

练习 3

题 1

答案选 C。

题 2

答案选 D。

题 3

答案选 A。

题 4

答案选 D。

【解析】（题 1—2）：

第 1 题的题干较长，所以大家需要认真和耐心地理解题目之后再思考：对照组联想到的单词比实验组少的原因是对照组更加可能怎么样？所以这道题主要是找到实验组和对照组出现不同实验结果的原因。那么我们可以从第 2 题的行号入手，判断哪个行号可以解释实验结果的差异。

第 2 题 A 选项 Lines 35–39 只是实验的过程，不是解释，排除。B 选项 Lines 42–43 是实验结果，但是不是原因，排除。C 选项 Lines 46–47 是实验结果，排除。D 选项 Lines 47–50 主要提到了实验组（Their ability 中的“他们的”指的是实验组）的学生联想单词的能力是来自他们减少了对无关信息的过滤。所以这个选项解释了为什么这些学生能够联想到更多单词。那么反过来推理，对照组关联的单词更少是因为过滤了很多信息。所以回到第 1 题，答案选择 C。

（题 3—4）：

第 3 题是一道态度题，所以我们可以按照先上题后下题的步骤进行解答。上面的题问的是作者认为大脑疲惫是因为什么。通过整篇文章的实验和观点来看，大脑疲惫会激发人的创造力，从态度性质上肯定是正面态度，其次和创造力相关，所以这道题可直接选择 A。接着根据第 3 题的答案进行下题的选择：a potential opportunity for creative inspiration that should be pursued. 答案关键词是 creative inspiration 以及 should be pursued，所以下题答案是 D。因为 D 选项中的 we should 是一种建议，后面的 creative genius 也正好对应 creative inspiration。

练习 4

题 1

答案选 A。

题 2

答案选 D。

题 3

答案选 B。

题 4

答案选 D。

【解析】（题 1—2）：

第 1 题题干关键词是 most researchers interested in skill acquisition，也就是问大部分研究人员对获得技巧感兴趣的原因。我们可以先看第二题行号。

第 2 题 A 选项提到了 researchers，研究人员把这种方法称作 blocking。但是第 1 题中没有选项对应，故排除。B 选项是对比 interleaving 和 blocking 两种练习方法，和 researchers 无关，所以排除。C 选项是举例说明什么是 interleaving 的练习方式，排除。D 选项提到居然很少有研究讨论 interleaving 在日常生活中的运用。也就是说，研究人员对日常生活中的 interleaving 方式并没有太多的兴趣。虽然这个选项没有直接提到 researchers 这个词，但是提到了 study，毕竟 study 是 researcher 开展的，所以其实是回答了上一题的问题。因此第 2 题选 D，第 1 题选择 A "unconcerned with the relevance of interleaving to people's routine activities".

（题 3—4）：

第 3 题是态度题，所以仍然可以采用先上题后下题的方式进行。根据文章实验结果可以看到 (Line 50)，采用 interleaving 的练习方式结果会更强、更稳定持久；另外，在文章最后一段总结中提到了虽然刚开始需要投入更多努力，但是结果更好。所以第 3 题选择 B 选项。再根据 B 选项的描述，选择最佳的同义转述的行号，于是第 4 题选择 D。

二、文章单独询证题

练习 1

这道题问的是下面哪个选项支持这样一个结论：Mr. Peters 想引起注意。那么关键词很清晰：Mr. Peters、attract attention。

根据关键词，我们看看选项即可判断：

A 选项，他没有意识到任何改变，这个和引起注意无关，排除。

B 选项，他有意识地紧了紧领带并做出一种手势从而邻桌的两位女士可以看到他手上的戒指。正确。

C 和 D 也可以排除。

练习 2

题目问哪个选项能够支持 20 行的 skeptics 的观点。首先看到 skeptics 的观点是：people's opinions are easily swayed by those of others。

接着看选项：

A 选项 55—58 行，这句话是实验结果，收到虚假正面投票评论的组相比对照组，更加有可能收到更多的正面评论，说明人们的观点会受到别人的影响，所以正确。

B 选项 58—60 行，如果是负面投票，则不会受到影响。

C 选项 63—65 行，此句转折，这样的实验结果对于负面操控是不成立的。

D 选项 76—79 行，这个选项貌似正确，但是注意说的是新闻的种类会影响到人们被操控的程度。但是题干说的是人们会受其他人的观点影响，而不是新闻的类型。

练习 3

题干问哪个选项支持文章的第一句话。文章第一句话是 Knowing your own reputation can be surprisingly difficult“想知道自己的声誉是非常难的”，再看选项。

A 选项，只是提到了一个研究，但没有研究结果，排除。

B 选项，在说明 correlation 的含义，而且是假设情况，排除。

C 选项，继续说明 correlation 的含义和作用。

D 选项，正确。尽管你认为同事认为你多有智慧，但是你很难知道哪一个同事认为你睿智，哪一个不这样认为。

第七章

语气识别与态度题

Tone: the mood or attitude conveyed by words or speech.

语气表达某个人对某件事或是其他人的看法和态度。简单来说，语气就是表达时候所展现的感情色彩。我们先通过一个具体例子来感受一下不同表达所体现的不同语气和态度。

首先，我们来假设一个场景：假期 Henson 去一个动物园游玩，但是发现动物园中洗手间非常少，于是他写了一封信给动物园管理处，给他们提建议。不久 Henson 收到了动物园的回信。下面有两封回信，我们来判断一下这两封的语气和背后的态度。

Letter A	Letter B
Dear Lake Park Zoo Visitor: Thank you for your letter. We will take your suggestion into consideration. We appreciate your feedback. Please visit us again soon.	Dear Henson: Thank you for your recent letter concerning the washing rooms in our zoo. We are taking your recommendation very seriously and truly appreciate your feedbace. We hope that you will visit us again soon.

咱们中国有个成语叫“言为心声”。在判断两封回信背后的语气时，大家可以先比较一下这两封信的 words and diction（措辞）。

1. Letter A 开头称呼 Zoo Visitor；Letter B 开头称呼具体名字。

2. Letter A 只说谢谢来信；而 Letter B 提到了具体的来信内容。

3. Letter B 中有两个强烈表达感情的副词：seriously 和 truly。

4. 最后的结尾同学们可以自己感受感情的不同。

所以我们可以得到结论：

The tone of letter A: uncaring, indifferent.

The tone of letter B: sincere, respectful.

我们再通过一个具体例子给大家展示不同的语气。

假设 6 个不同的人租了一所破烂的房屋居住，在入住时分别说了 6 句不同的话。大家可以看看这些句子的语气以及和下面这 6 个形容词如何匹配。

optimistic、painful、tolerant、sentimental、humorous、objective

1. This place may be shabby, but since both of my children were born here, it has a special place in my heart.

2. This isn’t the greatest apartment in the world, but it’s not really that bad.

3. If only there were some decent jobs out there, I wouldn't be reduced to living in this miserable dump.

4. This place does need some repairs, but I'm sure the landlord will be making improvements sometime soon.

5. When we move away, we're planning to release three hundred cockroaches and tow mice, so we can leave the place exactly as we found it.

6. This is the apartment we live in. It provides shelter.

句 1 表达了房屋虽然破烂不堪，但是因为孩子出生在此，所以也很特别。整体来看是正面态度，而且和孩子出生相关，情感上重要。所以是 sentimental，充满 feeling。

句 2 也是转折，虽然不是那么好，但是也没有那么糟糕，说明是可以忍受的。

句 3 表达了自己没有很好的工作，结果沦落至此，体现出非常痛苦的情感。

句 4 也含有转折，主要表达了相信房东会做些改进，对未来有所期待，所以是 optimistic。

句 5 是幽默的说法：将来离开的时候，抓几百只蟑螂和老鼠放进去，这样就和刚刚搬进来时一样了。用夸张的方式表达这所房子的破烂不堪，是幽默的语气。

句 6 没有任何情感词，完全是客观描述。

一、如何判断句子语气？

1. 情态动词

比如 must 表达确定，而 may 就是可能；need 表达要求（强制性），而 can 表达建议（选择性）。

2. 绝对词表达强烈语气

比如 never、impossible、only。

3. 带有情感的名词、动词、形容词

褒义词（commendatory term）表达正面肯定的态度；贬义词（derogatory term）表达负面否定的态度。

比如 His voice was so pure that it evoke beautiful pictures in our minds. 中的 pure、beautiful 都可以体现对这个人的仰慕态度（admiration）。

He is making a perfect idiot of himself. 这里的 idiot 表达出强烈的不满和鄙视态度。

4. 肢体语言展现态度

比如 shrug（耸肩）、frown（皱眉）、turn away（转身）等表示负面态度，可能是不在乎、冷漠、

反对、烦躁或者厌恶等。

outstretch one's hands (摊手) 大多表达无奈 (helpless) 。

smile (微笑) 、pat on the back/shoulder (拍后背 / 肩膀) 大多表达肯定和鼓励。

5. 直接给出情感或语气词

"She's a perfect girl," said Mr. Smith with great conviction. 这里直接表达非常确信。

SAT 考试常见语气态度词汇总。

类别	单词	含义
含 pass 的单词	passionate	*adj.* 热情的；易怒的；热烈的
	passive	*adj.* 消极的；被动的
	impassive	*adj.* 无感情的；无感觉的；冷淡的 the absence of any external sign of emotion in action or facial expression
	impassioned	*adj.* 激烈的 filled with passion or zeal: showing great warmth or intensity of feeling
	compassionate	*adj.* 有同情心的；慈悲的；怜悯的
	dispassionate	*adj.* 冷静的；不带偏见的；不动感情的 not influenced by strong feeling especially: not affected by personal or emotional involvement
含 path 的单词	apathetic	*adj.* 无动于衷的；缺乏兴趣的；缺乏感情的
	antipathetic	*adj.* 讨厌的；格格不入的 having a natural aversion
	sympathetic	*adj.* 有同情心的；赞成的；合意的 existing or operating through an affinity, interdependence, or mutual association
	pathos	*n.* 悲怆；同情；怜悯；痛苦 an element in experience or in artistic representation evoking pity or compassion
含 sent 的单词	sentimental	*adj.* 充满感情的；感情脆弱的
	consent	*n.* 同意；许可 *v.* 同意；答应；赞成
	dissent	*v.* 持异议；不同意
	sensitive	*adj.* 敏感的；神经过敏的；易受伤害的；易怒的
	sensible	*adj.* 有感觉的；明智的；有判断力的
	resent	*v.* 愤恨；怨恨；憎恶 to feel or express annoyance or ill will

有吸引力的，有魅力的	intriguing	*adj.* 有趣的 engaging the interest to a marked degree
	compelling	强迫性的；引人注目的 forceful，demanding attention
	inviting	*adj.* 引人注目的；诱人的
	alluring	*adj.* 诱惑的
	appealing	*adj.* 上诉的；有魅力的；哀求的；动人的
	tempting	*adj.* 诱惑人的；吸引人的
	fascinating	*adj.* 迷人的；着魔的；醉人的
	enthralling	*adj.* 迷人的；吸引人的
	entrancing	*adj.* 迷人的；吸引人的
	enticing	*adj.* 迷人的；吸引人的
坚定的	determined	*adj.* 坚决的；决意的
	resolute	*adj.* 坚决的；毅然的；刚毅的 marked by firm determination
	decisive	*adj.* 决定性的；果断的；坚定的
	adamant	*adj.* 坚硬无比的；固执的；坚定不移的
	unbending	*adj.* 不曲的；不屈的；坚决的
	steadfast	*adj.* 坚定的；固定的；踏实的
	persistent	*adj.* 坚持不懈的
	perseverant	*adj.* 坚持不懈的
	unyielding	yield 意为“屈服”，所以 unyielding 表示“不屈服的，坚定的”
犹豫的，不确定的	hesitant	*adj.* 迟疑的；犹豫不定的；踌躇的
	tentative	*adj.* 试验性的；暂时的 not fully worked out or developed; uncertain
	doubtful	*adj.* 可疑的；不确的；疑心的
	uncertain	*adj.* 无常的；不可预测的；不确定的
	diffident	*adj.* 无自信的，羞怯的 hesitant in acting or speaking through lack of self-confidence
	dubious	*adj.* 可疑的；不确定的 giving rise to uncertainty
公正的	neutral	*adj.* 中立的；无色的；中性的
	unbiased	*adj.* 无偏见的 free from all prejudice and favoritism
	impartial	*adj.* 公平的；不偏不倚的
	unprejudiced	*adj.* 无偏见的；公平的；没有成见的

<table>
<tr><th>类别</th><th>单词</th><th>含义</th></tr>
<tr><td rowspan="7">傲慢的</td><td>arrogant</td><td>adj. 傲慢的；自负的；自大的</td></tr>
<tr><td>haughty</td><td>adj. 傲慢的；自大的；骄傲的</td></tr>
<tr><td>cavalier</td><td>adj. 漫不经心的；傲慢的；无忧无虑的；目空一切的</td></tr>
<tr><td>superior</td><td>adj. 上好的；高傲的；出众的</td></tr>
<tr><td>overbearing</td><td>adj. 傲慢的；专横的；逞威风的；压倒性的</td></tr>
<tr><td>supercilious</td><td>adj. 自大的；目空一切的；傲慢的</td></tr>
<tr><td>insolent</td><td>adj. 粗野的；侮慢的；无礼的 insultingly contemptuous in speech or conduct</td></tr>
<tr><td rowspan="9">鄙视</td><td>scorn</td><td rowspan="9">synonyms SCOFF, JEER, GIBE, FLEER, SNEER, FLOUT mean to show one’s contempt in derision or mockery. SCOFF stresses insolence, disrespect, or incredulity as motivating the derision <scoffed at their concerns>. JEER suggests a coarser more undiscriminating derision <the crowd jeered at the prisoners>. GIBE implies taunting either good-naturedly or in sarcastic derision <hooted and gibed at the umpire>. FLEER suggests grinning or grimacing derisively <the saucy jackanapes fleered at my credulity>. SNEER stresses insulting by contemptuous facial expression, phrasing, or tone of voice <sneered at anything romantic>. FLOUT stresses contempt shown by refusal to heed <flouted the conventions of polite society>.</td></tr>
<tr><td>sniff</td></tr>
<tr><td>sneer</td></tr>
<tr><td>contempt</td></tr>
<tr><td>jeer</td></tr>
<tr><td>disdain</td></tr>
<tr><td>despise</td></tr>
<tr><td>spurn</td></tr>
<tr><td>mock</td></tr>
<tr><td rowspan="10">赞美; 赞扬;
尊重</td><td>admire</td><td rowspan="10">synonyms REVERE, REVERENCE, VENERATE, WORSHIP, ADORE mean to honor and admire profoundly and respectfully. REVERE stresses deference and tenderness of feeling <a professor revered by her students>. REVERENCE presupposes an intrinsic merit and inviolability in the one honored and a similar depth of feeling in the one honoring <reverenced the academy’s code of honor>. VENERATE implies a holding as holy or sacrosanct because of character, association, or age <heroes still venerated>. WORSHIP implies homage usually expressed in words or ceremony <worships their memory>. ADORE implies love and stresses the notion of an individual and personal attachment <we adored our doctor>.</td></tr>
<tr><td>respect</td></tr>
<tr><td>revere</td></tr>
<tr><td>laud</td></tr>
<tr><td>applaude</td></tr>
<tr><td>praise</td></tr>
<tr><td>accolade</td></tr>
<tr><td>acclaim</td></tr>
<tr><td>venerate</td></tr>
<tr><td>adore</td></tr>
</table>

喜悦的；高兴的	delighted	*adj.* 高兴的；愉快的
	pleased	
	cheerful	
	exhilarated	
	ebullient	
	satisfied	
悲伤；沮丧	sorrow	synonyms SORROW, GRIEF, ANGUISH, WOE, REGRET mean distress of mind. SORROW implies a sense of loss or a sense of guilt and remorse <a family united in sorrow upon the patriarch's death>. GRIEF implies poignant sorrow for an immediate cause <the inexpressible grief of the bereaved parents>. ANGUISH suggests torturing grief or dread <the anguish felt by the parents of the kidnapped child>. WOE is deep or inconsolable grief or misery <cries of woe echoed throughout the bombed city>. REGRET implies pain caused by deep disappointment, fruitless longing, or unavailing remorse <nagging regret for missed opportunities>.
	grief	
	distress	
	depression	
	anguish	
	woe	
	dismay	
	dreary	
	sullen	
	agony	
启迪的；启发的	inspirational	*adj.* 有灵感的；鼓舞人心的
	enlightening	*adj.* 启迪的
	instructive	*adj.* 教导的；有益的
	illuminating	*adj.* 照明的；启蒙的
可笑的	ridiculous	synonyms LAUGHABLE, LUDICROUS, RIDICULOUS, COMIC, COMICAL mean provoking laughter or mirth. LAUGHABLE applies to anything occasioning laughter <laughable attempts at skating>. LUDICROUS suggests absurdity that excites both laughter and scorn <a thriller with a ludicrous plot>. RIDICULOUS suggests extreme absurdity, foolishness, or contemptibility <a ridiculous display of anger>. COMIC applies especially to what arouses thoughtful amusement <a comic character>. COMICAL applies to what arouses spontaneous hilarity <a comical hat>.
	ludicrous	
	laughable	
	comic	
	absurd	

<table>
<tr><td rowspan="4">胆小；害怕</td><td>timid</td><td>adj. 胆小的；羞怯的</td></tr>
<tr><td>trepid</td><td>adj. 胆小的；羞怯的</td></tr>
<tr><td>intimidating</td><td>adj. 吓人的；令人生畏的</td></tr>
<tr><td>apprehensive</td><td>adj. 害怕的；惴惴不安的</td></tr>
<tr><td rowspan="5">疑惑；困惑</td><td>puzzle</td><td>v. 使迷惑；苦思而得出；使为难</td></tr>
<tr><td>baffle</td><td>v. 使困惑；使受挫折；难住</td></tr>
<tr><td>confuse</td><td>v. 搞乱；使糊涂</td></tr>
<tr><td>perplex</td><td>v. 使困惑；使复杂化</td></tr>
<tr><td>confound</td><td>v. 使混淆；挫败；使狼狈</td></tr>
<tr><td rowspan="6">谨慎；防卫</td><td>guarded</td><td rowspan="6">synonyms CAUTIOUS, CIRCUMSPECT, WARY, CHARY mean prudently watchful and discreet in the face of danger or risk. CAUTIOUS implies the exercise of forethought usually prompted by fear of danger <a cautious driver>. CIRCUMSPECT suggests less fear and stresses the surveying of all possible consequences before acting or deciding <circumspect in his business dealings>. WARY emphasizes suspiciousness and alertness in watching for danger and cunning in escaping it <keeps a wary eye on the competition>. CHARY implies a cautious reluctance to give, act, or speak freely <chary of signing papers without having read them first>.</td></tr>
<tr><td>cautious</td></tr>
<tr><td>wary</td></tr>
<tr><td>circumspect</td></tr>
<tr><td>reserved</td></tr>
<tr><td>prudent</td></tr>
<tr><td rowspan="6">愤怒；气愤</td><td>rage</td><td rowspan="6">synonyms IRRITATE, EXASPERATE, NETTLE, PROVOKE, RILE, PEEVE mean to excite a feeling of anger or annoyance. IRRITATE implies a gradual arousing of angry feelings that may range from mere impatience to rage <constant nagging that irritated me greatly>. EXASPERATE suggests galling annoyance and the arousing of extreme impatience <his exasperating habit of putting off needed decisions>. NETTLE suggests a sharp but passing annoyance or stinging <your pompous attitude nettled several people>. PROVOKE implies an arousing of strong annoyance that may excite to action <remarks made solely to provoke her>. RILE implies inducing an angry or resentful agitation <the new work schedules riled the employees>. PEEVE suggests arousing fretful often petty or querulous irritation <a toddler peeved at being refused a cookie>.</td></tr>
<tr><td>outrage</td></tr>
<tr><td>wrath</td></tr>
<tr><td>irritation</td></tr>
<tr><td>indignation</td></tr>
<tr><td>vexation</td></tr>
</table>

讽刺的	ironic	synonyms SARCASTIC, SATIRIC, IRONIC, SARDONIC mean marked by bitterness and a power or will to cut or sting. SARCASTIC implies an intentional inflicting of pain by deriding, taunting, or ridiculing <a critic known for his sarcastic remarks>. SATIRIC implies that the intent of the ridiculing is censure and reprobation <a satiric look at contemporary society>. IRONIC implies an attempt to be amusing or provocative by saying usually the opposite of what is meant <made the ironic observation that the government could always be trusted>. SARDONIC implies scorn, mockery, or derision that is manifested by either verbal or facial expression <surveyed the scene with a sardonic smile>.
	satirical	
	mocking	
	sardonic	
	sarcastic	
怀疑的	distrustful	*adj.* 不信任的；怀疑的
	suspicious	*adj.* 可疑的；怀疑的；疑惧的
	skeptical	*adj.* 怀疑论的；不可知论的；怀疑的
其他	cynical	*adj.* 愤世嫉俗的；冷嘲的；讽刺的 having a sneering disbelief in sincerity or integrity
	resigned	*adj.* 认命的；听任的；服从的 to give (oneself) over without resistance <resigned herself to her fate>
	dismissive	*adj.* 轻视的；轻蔑的；不尊重的；不感兴趣的 to reject serious consideration of <dismissed the thought>
	condescend	*v.* 傲慢；屈尊 to assume an air of superiority
	pragmatic	*adj.* 切合实际的；务实的；行得通的
	practical	*adj.* 实际的；实用性的；现实的
	theoretical	*adj.* 理论上的；空谈的
	wistful	*adj.* 忧伤的；渴望的 full of yearning or desire tinged with melancholy also : inspiring such yearning <a wistful memoir>
	ambivalent	*adj.* 有矛盾情绪的 simultaneous and contradictory attitudes or feelings
	critical	*adj.* 批评的；危险的；决定性的；临界的

	emphatic	*adj.* 强调的；加强语气的 uttered with or marked by emphasis
	conviction	*n.* 定罪；坚信；信服 a firmly held belief
	admonish	*v.* 告诫；提醒；警告；劝告 a : to indicate duties or obligations to b : to express warning or disapproval to especially in a gentle, earnest, or solicitous manner
	solicitous	*adj.* 热心的；热切期望的；渴望的

二、句子语气分析

1. It wasn't a question of whether we'd make it; we'd conquered that years before.

【解析】句子中有 conquer "战胜" 这个单词，可以看出作者的语气是有信心和骄傲。

Tone: confidence and pride

2. Mom said, "Aren't you excited about having another big sister?" Kevin just shrugged and acted bored

【解析】Kevin 的回应主要是动作 shrug（耸肩），另外直接给出态度是 bored（厌烦的）。

Tone: indifference and bored

3. The idea that the number of people per square mile is a key determinant of population pressure is as widespread as it is wrong.

【解析】句子说明一个观点是错误的（wrong），所以有否定语气；此外，还说这种错误是 widespread（普遍的），所以表示强调。

Tone: critical and emphatic

4. You could easily miss the building if you didn't know what you were looking for. But once you were inside, you could never mistake it for anything else.

【解析】句子中有转折逻辑，后面重点表达了 never mistake，流露出确信的语气。

Tone: conviction

5. Many say that since making music is an art, artists like me should do it simply for the love of it. But how free can artists be to do what we love if we must spend most of our days doing something else to make a living?

【解析】句子是转折逻辑，所以有否定和批评前句观点（反驳艺术家就应该因为热爱而进行艺术创作）。之后用反问（rhetorical question）进行强调，艺术家也要考虑生计问题（make a living）。所以整个语气是批判、现实以及强调。

Tone: critical, realistic, emphatic

6. Remember, you need to be home by ten o'clock.

【解析】句子中含有必须（need to），表达要求。

Tone: mandatory and bossy

二、段落语气分析

例 1

Some people boast of having a sixth sense, professing to know or see things that others cannot. Fortune-tellers, mind readers, and mystics all lay claim to this power, and, in so doing, elicit widespread fascination in others, especially book publishers and television producers. The questionable field of parapsychology is of course founded on the belief that at least some people actually possess this mysterious power. But to me, the real mystery is why so many fortunetellers choose to work the phones on television psychic hotlines instead of becoming insanely wealthy stock traders on Wall Street.

What is the tone of the last sentence?

【解析】有些人声称自己有第六感，能够感知别人不知道的东西。但作者觉得他们为什么不去华尔街预测，然后一夜暴富呢？所以最后一句是以幽默的方式讽刺这些人。

Tone: critical and ironic

例 2

I saw it first in early summer. It was a green and sleeping bud, raising itself toward the sun. Over the summer this sunflower grew to a plant of incredible beauty, turning its face daily toward the sun, in community with rain, mineral, mountain air, and sand.

What is the author's tone in describing this paragraph?

【解析】文章描述的是植物的生长，用了 incredible 这种正面的形容词；另外，文章使用拟人（personification）的方式描写嫩芽的生长，体现对自然生物的惊奇和欣赏。

Tone: informal and admiration

例 3

Ever since I became a published writer, my family had been trying to figure out where the writing talent came from. "Experience has given her the inspiration," one uncle claimed. Another uncle believed that probably I got the writing genes from my father.

What are her uncles' tone?

【解析】文章描写了 uncles 对于我写作能力的来源作出推测，含不确定的语气。

Tone: speculative and uncertain

例 4

And now it was only four days before he would be back in that same village. He was excited, and at the same time uneasy: maybe the girl had already forgotten him. Lot of shepherds passed through, selling their wool.

"It doesn't matter," he said to his sheep. "I know other girls in other places."

What is the boy's tone when he said "It doesn't matter"?

【解析】上文直接提到小男孩的情感——兴奋而又不安，害怕女孩已经忘记他了。后文提到没有关系，是一种自我安慰的语气。

Tone: self-comforting

例 5

In spite of an endless stream of frustrating obstacles, victories have been won and despair has given way to hope. Farm workers unionized several ranches and have shouted "no" to the paternalism and exploitation of their bosses. They now have improved wages and working conditions. They have developed inspiring leadership among themselves on their ranches. They have learned the machinery of unionism; grievance procedures, negotiations, and the new sense of dignity and power every man needs in order to face the future.

What is the tone of this paragraph?

【解析】文章关键词——victories、improved、inspiring。段落呈现让步关系：尽管有很多障碍，但是赢得了胜利，希望取代了绝望。后续描写了工人们的各种积极进步。所以语气是乐观和情绪高涨。

Tone: optimistic and up-lifted

三、官方试题分析

例 1

（试题选自 www.khanacademy.org）

This little attendrissement, with the solitude of my walk led me into a train of reflections on that unequal division of property which occasions the numberless instances of wretchedness which I had observed in this country and is to be observed all over Europe. The property of this country is absolutely concentered in a very few hands, having revenues of from half a million of guineas a year downwards. These employ the flower of the country as servants, some of them having as many as 200 domestics, not labouring. They employ also a great number of manufacturers, and tradesmen, and lastly the class of labouring husbandmen. But after all these comes the most numerous of all the classes, that is, the poor who cannot find work.

What main effect does the phrase "flower of the country" have on the tone of the passage?

A) It lightens the tone by providing a metaphor of beauty in an otherwise bleak narrative.

B) It provides an impassioned tone to describe the discrepancy between the relative privilege of the few and the hardship of the many.

C) It creates a tone of praise by comparing the workers of France to those in the U.S.

D) It creates an optimistic tone by showing that the people of France are variously employed.

【解析】这里 flower of the country 指的是被少数富人所雇佣的劳动者；而这句话主要体现出贫富差距之大。所以答案选 B——激烈的情感表达出少数人的特权和大多数人的艰辛的巨大反差。

例 2

（试题选自 www.khanacademy.org）

In fact, in October [2004], French researchers announced findings that illustrate afresh just how close some viruses might come. Didier Raoult and his colleagues at the University of the Mediterranean in Marseille announced that they had sequenced the genome of the largest known virus,Mimivirus, which was discovered in 1992. The virus, about the same size as a small bacterium, infects amoebae.Sequence analysis of the virus revealed numerous genes previously thought to exist only in cellular organisms. Some of these genes are involved in making the proteins encoded by the viral DNA and may make it easier for Mimivirus toco-opt host cell replication systems. As the research team noted in its report in the journal *Science*, the enormous complexity of the Mimivirus's genetic complement challenges the established frontier between viruses and parasitic cellular organisms.

Which choice best describes the author's tone in describing the research described in the paragraph?

A) Analytical

B) Ambivalent

C) Biased

D) Objective

【解析】这个段落主要是描述一些科学家的研究和结论，但是并没有任何评价，完全呈现发生的事实。所以选 D“客观的”（objective）。

例 3

（试题选自 The SAT Practice Test 8）

The Venus flytrap [Dionaea muscipula] needs to know when an ideal meal is crawling across its leaves.Closing its trap requires a huge expense of energy,and reopening the trap can take several hours, so Dionaea only wants to spring closed when it's sure that the dawdling insect visiting its surface is large enough to be worth its time. The large black hairs on their lobes allow the Venus fly traps to literally feel their prey, and they act as triggers that spring the trap closed when the proper prey makes its way across the trap. If the insect touches just one hair, the trap will not spring shut; but a large enough bug will likely touch two hairs within about twenty seconds,and that signal springs the Venus flytrap into action.

We can look at this system as analogous to short-term memory. First, the flytrap encodes the information (forms the memory) that something (it doesn't know what) has touched one of its hairs.Then it stores this information for a number of seconds (retains the memory) and finally retrieves this information (recalls the memory) once a second hair is touched. If a small ant takes a while to get from one hair to the next, the trap will have forgotten the first touch by the time the ant brushes up against the next hair. In other words, it loses the storage of the information, doesn't close, and the an thappily meanders on. How does the plant encode and store the information from the unassuming bug's encounter with the first hair? How does it remember the first touch in order to react upon the second?

The use of the phrases "dawdling insect", "happily meanders", and "unassuming bug's encounter" in the first two paragraphs establishes a tone that is

A) academic.

B) melodramatic.

C) informal.

D) mocking.

【解析】从用词上，dawdle（闲逛）、happily meanders（开心地漫步）、unassuming bug（低调的昆虫）都是采用拟人的修辞手法。

选项 A，学术的，错误；因为这里是拟人的修辞手法，生动形象地展现昆虫在叶子上的活动，并非学术性的。

选项 B，音乐剧的，戏剧性的，错误；这里并没有夸张或情节的曲折。

选项 C，正确；这里是非正式的语气，比较随意，甚至有点轻松幽默。

选项 D，错误，没有嘲笑任何事物。

四、语气题练习

1. Why is Venus so unlike Earth? The answer can only lie in its lesser distance from the Sun. It seems that in the early days of the solar system the Sun was less luminous than it is now, in which Case Venus and Earth may have started to evolve along the same lines, but when the Sun became more powerful the whole situation changed. Earth, at 93 million miles, was just out of harm's way, but Venus,at 67 million, was not. The water in oceans vaporized, the carbonates were driven out of the rocks, and in a relatively short time on the cosmic scale, Venus was transformed from a potentially life-bearing world into the inferno of today.

The tone of the statemen ("The answer...Sun") is best described as

A) regretful

B) guarded

C) skeptical

D) decisive

2. Many say that since making music is an art, artists like me should do it simply for the love of it. But how free can artists be to do what we love if we must spend most of our days doing something else to make a living?

The tone of the statemen ("But how…a living?") is best described as

A) resolute

B) eager

C) resigned

D) cavalier

3. Finally, one evening at teatime, gauging the psychological moment, Nawab asked if he might say a word. The landowner, who was cheerfully filing his nails in front of a crackling rosewood fire, told him to go ahead.

"Sir, as you know, your lands stretch from here to the Indus, and on these lands are fully seventeen tube wells, and to tend these seventeen tube wells there is but one man, me, your servant. In your service I have earned these gray hairs" —here he bowed his head to show the gray— "and now I cannot fulfill my duties as I should. Enough, sir, enough. I beg you, forgive me my weakness. Better a darkened house and proud hunger within than disgrace in the light of day. Release me, I ask you, I beg you."

The tone of Nawab's words is best described as

A) respectful

B) humourous

C) timid

D) furious

4. Then the work began. The man was indefatigable. He was like the spirit of energy. He was in very place about the stage at once, leading the chorus, showing them steps, twisting some awkward girl into shape, shouting, gesticulating, abusing the pianist.

"Now, now," he would shout. "the left foot on that beat. Bah, bah, stop! You walk like a lot of tin soilders. Are your joints rusty? Do you want oil?"

The tone of the statement ("Are your joints rusty? Do you want oil?") is best described as

A) scornful

B) cheerful

C) respectful

D) indifferent

五、语气题练习答案与解析

1. 为什么金星不像地球？ The answer can only lie in its lesser distance from the Sun. 题目问的是第二句的语气是什么。这个句子首先给出了前面问题的答案，其次句子有 only 这个绝对词，表达了对答案的确信。所以语气是确信的、肯定的。选择 D。

2. 很多人认为音乐是艺术，所以艺术家应该完全是为了爱而进行创作。But how free can artists be to do what we love if we must spend most of our days doing something else to make a

living? 题目问第二句话的语气是什么。根据这个句子的意思可以知道是反问，也就是不太认同第一句的观点。同时也表达出如果艺术家为了生计挣扎是不可能做自己喜欢的事情的无奈情感。所以答案选择 C “resigned”（无奈的）。

3. 从 Nawab 所说的大段文字来看，很多地方体现出语气和态度。比如用了很多次 sir，表达尊敬；比如用了 beg，表达请求；用了 forgive my weakness，表达谦卑。所以最佳答案是 A。

4. 这句话从文章来看应该是一个艺术团的指导者说的，而且可以看出来用有点讽刺和挖苦的语气来批判这些学生。所以答案选择 A。

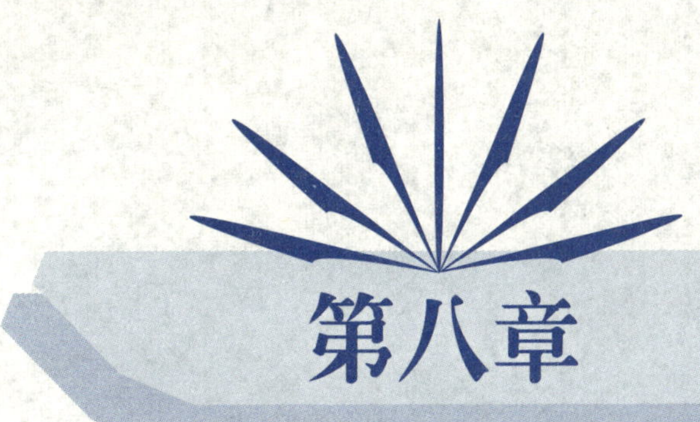

第八章

历史类文章的长难句与段落结构

SAT SAT SAT SAT SAT SAT SAT SAT SAT SAT SAT SAT SAT SAT SAT SAT SAT

试想在考试中看到的历史类文章是这样的：

Fellow-Citizens of the Senate and of the House of Representatives:

Among the vicissitudes incident to life no event could have filled me with greater anxieties than that of which the notification was transmitted by your order, and received on the 14th day of the present month. On the one hand, I was summoned by my Country, whose voice I can never hear but with veneration and love, from a retreat which I had chosen with the fondest predilection, and, in my flattering hopes, with an immutable decision, as the asylum of my declining years—a retreat which was rendered every day more necessary as well as more dear to me by the addition of habit to inclination, and of frequent interruptions in my health to the gradual waste committed on it by time. On the other hand, the magnitude and difficulty of the trust to which the voice of my country called me, being sufficient to awaken in the wisest and most experienced of her citizens a distrustful scrutiny into his qualifications, could not but overwhelm with despondence one who (inheriting inferior endowments from nature and unpracticed in the duties of civil administration) ought to be peculiarly conscious of his own deficiencies. In this conflict of emotions all I dare aver is that it has been my faithful study to collect my duty from a just appreciation of every circumstance by which it might be affected. All I dare hope is that if, in executing this task, I have been too much swayed by a grateful remembrance of former instances, or by an affectionate sensibility to this transcendent proof of the confidence of my fellow-citizens, and have thence too little consulted my incapacity as well as disinclination for the weighty and untried cares before me, my error will be palliated by the motives which mislead me, and its consequences be judged by my country with some share of the partiality in which they originated.

大部分同学内心肯定会想“这……也太难了吧，这次要挂了……”，确实，大部分同学觉得历史类文章难主要原因是句子太长或写得太晦涩。另外，很多熟词僻义和生词导致理解上的难度很大。如果想准确清晰地理解历史类文章的观点和细节，首先要从句子理解上克服重重障碍。

历史类文章句子障碍 1——长句

在历史类文章中，经常会出现一句话超过 40 个单词的情况。比如：

Who can say whether, as time goes on, we may not dress in military uniform, with gold lace on our breasts, swords at our sides, and something like the old family coal-scuttle on our heads, save that that venerable object was never decorated with plumes of white horsehair. (48 words) The SAT Practice Test 1

The male element has held high carnival thus far; it has fairly run riot from the beginning, overpowering the feminine element everywhere, crushing out all the diviner qualities in human nature, until we know but little of true manhood and womanhood, of the latter comparatively nothing, for it has scarce been recognized as a power until within the last century. (60 words) The SAT Practice Test 2

Consider—I address you as a legislator—whether, when men contend for their freedom, and to be allowed to judge for themselves respecting their own happiness, it be not inconsistent and unjust to subjugate women, even though you firmly believe that you are acting in the manner best calculated to promote their happiness? (53 words) The SAT Practice Test 3

To avoid...the evils of inconstancy and versatility, ten thousand times worse than those of obstinacy and the blindest prejudice, we have consecrated the state, that no man should approach to look into its defects or corruptions but with due caution; that he should never dream of beginning its reformation by its subversion; that he should approach to the faults of the state as to the wounds of a father, with pious awe and trembling solicitude. (76 words) The SAT Practice Test 4

所以，从上面可以看到几乎每篇文章都会有类似这样的长句。那么如何理解这些长句呢？

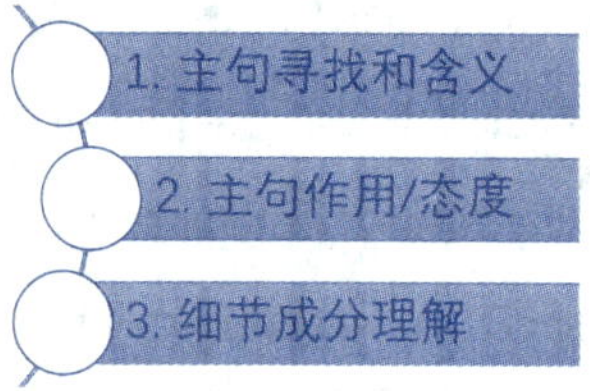
1. 主句寻找和含义
2. 主句作用/态度
3. 细节成分理解

1. 主句寻找和含义

大家可以自行回忆自己在备考托福时候寻找主句的方法。简单来说，就是忽略从句（定语从句、状语从句、同位语从句）、非谓语动词、插入语、介词短语等修饰成分即可。另外，历史类文章长句中的介词短语，基本上看到就可以跳过去。

2. 主句的作用或态度

找到主句之后，理解其意思，判断句子的作用。

3. 细节成分理解

之后再进行细节成分的补充理解，比如对各个从句、插入语等的理解。

一、历史类文章长句例题

例 1

When in the course of human events, it becomes necessary for one people to dissolve the political bands which have connected them with another, and to assume among the powers of the earth, the separate and equal station to which the laws of Nature and of Nature’s God entitle them, a decent respect to the opinions of mankind requires that they should declare the causes which impel them to the separation.

Adopted from *The Declaration of Independence*

(1) 主句寻找和含义

寻找这句话的主句其实还是有点难度的，主要在于前面的 when，大多数同学会认为和 in the course of human events 是一起的，it becomes necessary for one people to... 是主句。这样理解就错了。

细心的话会发现后面还有完整的一句话：a decent respect to the opinions of mankind requires that they should declare the causes. 这句话才是主句。前面的 when 其实引导的是 it becomes… entitle them，把前面语序变化一下大家就更容易理解。

In the course of human events, when it becomes…, a decent…

找到主句之后就是理解其意思：出于对人类情感的尊重，他们应该宣布原因（促使他们独立的原因）。在理解这句话的时候其实还存在一个疑问：他们是谁？根据代词的指代对象，应该往前去寻找，可以得知 they 指的是 one people，一个民族（根据语境，因为是《独立宣言》，指的是美国人民）。

(2) 主句的作用和功能

这是《独立宣言》的首段，也是首句，应该引出《独立宣言》的内容。既然主句应该指出独立的原因，所以这句话的作用就是引出独立的原因（introduce the reasons for the separation），也就是为什么要独立。

(3) 细节成分理解

前面是 when 引导的状语从句：在人类事件的发展过程中，当一个民族认为有必要去解除和另外一个民族直接的政治关联，并按照自然法则和上帝的旨意，以独立平等的身份立于世界之林时……

when 后面的从句主要是 it becomes necessary for…to do and to do 结构。从句中又包含两个定语从句（which have connected them with another）（to which the laws of Nature and of Nature's God entitle them）。

到此，就能完整理解句子的意思了。

在人类事件的发展过程中，当一个民族认为有必要去解除和另外一个民族直接的政治关联，并按照自然法则和上帝的旨意，以独立平等的身份立于世界之林时，出于对人类情感的尊重，他们应该宣布促使他们独立的原因。

例 2

When we recognize that in the federal government, with its millions of employees, there are but five hundred and thirty-seven elected officials, put into office to carry out the "will" of a people who for the most part know little and care less about the technical functioning of their government, the absurdity of the notion of rapid democratic responsiveness becomes clear.

(1) 主句寻找和含义

这句话和例 1 比较类似的地方在于前面也是 when 引导的状语从句。所以主句大家应该能够确认是：the absurdity of the notion of rapid democratic responsiveness becomes clear。

含义：民主体制能够迅速反应的观点的荒谬性就太明显了。

(2) 主句的作用和态度

对民主迅速反应这种观念或观点进行批判 (criticize the notion of rapid democratic responsiveness)。

(3) 细节成分理解

当我们意识到在联邦政府当中，有几百万的员工，有 537 位被选举的官员的时候 (这些当选官员来实施人民的“意愿”，而人民大部分情况下不知道也不关心这个政府的技术功能)。

例 3

Among the vicissitudes incident to life no event could have filled me with greater anxieties than that of which the notification was transmitted by your order, and received on the 14th day of the present month.

(1) 主句寻找和含义

这句话的主句是比较容易寻找的：no event could have filled me with greater anxieties than that (没有任何事情比那个给我带来更多的焦虑了 / 那个事情给我带来最大的焦虑)

(2) 主句的作用和功能

表达对这个事情的态度，而且是负面态度 (anxiety)。

(3) 细节成分理解

句子开头是介词短语：Among the vicissitudes incident to life. (在生活的沉浮当中)

之后是修饰 that 的定语从句 of which the notification was transmitted by your order, and received on the 14th day of the present month，具体说明这个事件是人民给华盛顿的通知 (就职总统)，以及在本月 14 日收到的通知。

所以整个句子的意思就是华盛顿得知自己就职总统，其实内心非常焦虑。

例 4

On the one hand, I was summoned by my Country, whose voice I can never hear but with veneration and love, from a retreat which I had chosen with the fondest predilection, and, in my flattering hopes, with an immutable decision, as the asylum of my declining years—a retreat which was rendered every day more necessary as well as more dear to me by the addition of habit to inclination, and of frequent interruptions in my health to the gradual waste committed on it by time.

(1) 主句寻找和含义

主句：I was summoned by my Country

后面接着是定语从句修饰 country (whose voice I can never hear but with veneration and love)，再接着是介词短语 (from a retreat)，retreat 后面是定语从句 (which I had chosen with the fondest predilection, and, in my flattering hopes, with an immutable decision, as the asylum of my declining years)，破折号后的句子作进一步补充说明 (—a retreat which was rendered every day more necessary as well as more dear to me by the addition of habit to inclination, and of frequent interruptions in my health to the gradual waste committed on it by time)

句子主干意思非常简单：我被国家召唤。

(2) 主句的作用和功能

那么，这样简单的一句话的作用是什么呢？其实如果和上句放在一起理解就很简单了。

"我对就任总统感到非常焦虑。一方面……"

其实只要看到一方面，就能理解这里是给出原因——我为什么感到焦虑。

(3) 细节成分理解

这句话细节非常多：

(whose voice I can never hear but with veneration and love) 修饰国家，表达华盛顿对国家的崇敬与热爱。

(from a retreat which I had chosen with the fondest predilection, and, in my flattering hopes, with an immutable decision, as the asylum of my declining years) 注意这里 retreat 的意思为 retiring (退休)。他本来想退休，而且带着热烈的倾向选择退休，希望能把退隐作为自己余生的安排。

(—a retreat which was rendered every day more necessary as well as more dear to me by the addition of habit to inclination, and of frequent interruptions in my health to the gradual waste committed on it by time) 继续对退隐进行说明：感觉退隐的必要性与日俱增。

二、历史类文章长句练习

1. On the other hand, the magnitude and difficulty of the trust to which the voice of my country called me, being sufficient to awaken in the wisest and most experienced of her citizens a distrustful scrutiny into his qualifications, could not but overwhelm with despondence one who (inheriting inferior endowments from nature and unpracticed in the duties of civil administration) ought to be peculiarly conscious of his own deficiencies.

2. Independent of the opinions of many great authors, that a free elective government cannot

be extended over large territories, a few reflections must evince, that one government and general legislation alone, never can extend equal benefits to all parts of the United States: Different laws, customs, and opinions exist in the different states, which by a uniform system of laws would be unreasonably invaded.

3. But it is nevertheless a maxim well established by experience, and generally acknowledged, where there has been sufficient experience, that the aggregate prosperity of manufactures, and the aggregate prosperity of Agriculture are intimately connected.

Alexander Hamilton, "Report on Manufactures"

4. When human beings are regarded as moral beings, sex, instead of being enthroned upon the summit, administering upon rights and responsibilities, sinks into insignificance and nothingness.

5. The Americans have applied to the sexes the great principle of political economy which governs the manufactures of our age, by carefully dividing the duties of man from those of woman, in order that the great work of society may be better carried on.

三、历史类文章长句练习解析

1. On the other hand, the magnitude and difficulty of the trust to which the voice of my country called me, being sufficient to awaken in the wisest and most experienced of her citizens a distrustful scrutiny into his qualifications, could not but overwhelm with despondence one who (inheriting inferior endowments from nature and unpracticed in the duties of civil administration) ought to be peculiarly conscious of his own deficiencies.

主干：The magnitude and difficulty of the trust could not but overwhelm with despondence one.

意思是：大家信任的广度和难度足以让一个人倍感压力而感到沮丧。

其他插入语和定语从句大家可以自行理解。

2. Independent of the opinions of many great authors, that a free elective government cannot be extended over large territories, a few reflections must evince, that one government and general legislation alone, never can extend equal benefits to all parts of the United States: Different laws, customs, and opinions exist in the different states, which by a uniform system of laws would be unreasonably invaded.

主 干：a few reflections must evince, that one government and general legislation alone, never can extend equal benefits to all parts of the United States.

意思是：一个整体的政府和立法是不可能给美国所有的部分相同的利益的。

3. But it is nevertheless a maxim well established by experience, and generally acknowledged, where there has been sufficient experience, that the aggregate prosperity of manufactures, and the

aggregate prosperity of Agriculture are intimately connected.

主干：it is nevertheless a maxim that the aggregate prosperity of manufactures, and the aggregate prosperity of Agriculture are intimately connected.

意思是：这是个真理：制造业和农业的整体繁荣是紧密相连的。

4. When human beings are regarded as moral beings, sex, instead of being enthroned upon the summit, administering upon rights and responsibilities, sinks into insignificance and nothingness.

主干：sex sinks into insignificance and nothingness.

意思是：性别无关紧要。

5. The Americans have applied to the sexes the great principle of political economy which governs the manufactures of our age, by carefully dividing the duties of man from those of woman, in order that the great work of society may be better carried on.

主干是：The Americans have applied to the sexes the great principle.

意思是：美国人把这个伟大的原则运用到性别上。

细节部分解释了原则是什么：细心区分男性和女性的职责，以便于社会的工作更好地进行下去。

历史类文章句子障碍 2——反问句

反问是用疑问的形式表达确定的意思，以加重语气的一种修辞手法。反问句表面看来是疑问的形式，但实际上表达的是肯定的意思，答案就在问句之中。反问的形式比一般的陈述句语气更加强烈，强调作者的观点。

反问句明知故问：看似疑问，其实是强调。

理解反问句的方法：反问句变成陈述句。真实含义一般是否定原句，比如：

反问句“SAT 不难吗？”其实表达“SAT 很难”；

反问句“托福不简单吗？”其实表达“托福很简单”；

反问句“他有什么资格这么说？”其实表达“他没有资格这么说”；

反问句“你觉得有问题吗？”其实表达“你不应该觉得有问题”；

反问句“你为什么喜欢他？”其实表达“你不应该喜欢他”。

一、反问句例题

例 1

Should the people of America divide themselves into three or four nations, would not the same thing happen? Would not similar jealousies arise, and be in like manner cherished?

Federalist Paper No. 5, published in 1787

开头的 should 其实是虚拟语气的省略用法，可还原为：If the people of America should divide themselves into three or four nations.

之后是两个反问句，变成陈述句是：

the same thing would happen. Similar jealousies would arise, and would be in like manner cherished.

句子整体意思就是：如果美国人民分裂成三四个国家，相同的事情会发生；国家之间会产生嫉妒。

例 2

The most sanguine advocates for three or four confederacies cannot reasonably suppose that they would long remain exactly on an equal footing in point of strength, even if it was possible

to form them so at first; but, admitting that to be practicable, yet what human contrivance can secure the continuance of such equality?

Federalist Paper No. 5, published in 1787

反问句：yet what human contrivance can secure the continuance of such equality?

陈述句：no human contrivance can secure the continuance of such equality.

最热心的推崇三四个邦联国家的人不能够合理地期待这些国家会长期保持平等的力量；即使刚开始可能这样，但是有什么人类的计策能够确保这种平等的持续呢？（没有任何计策能够确保）

例 3

Is it not apparent, that their delicate constitutions, their peaceful inclinations, and the many duties of motherhood, set them apart from strenuous habits and onerous duties, and summon them to gentle occupations and the cares of the home?

反问句：Is it not apparent that…?

陈述句：It is apparent that…

这个是很明显的事情：女性纤弱的身体、平和的性格以及母亲的职责使她们与沉重的工作分开，让她们从事轻松的工作和照顾家庭。

例 4

Consider whether, when men contend for their freedom, and to be allowed to judge for themselves respecting their own happiness, it be not inconsistent and unjust to subjugate women, even though you firmly believe that you are acting in the manner best calculated to promote their happiness?

这句话首先是长句，所以我们按照长句的处理方法先找出主干。

(when men contend for their freedom, and to be allowed to judge for themselves respecting their own happiness) 为状语从句，充当插入语。

(even though you firmly believe that you are acting in the manner best calculated to promote their happiness) 是让步状语从句。

所以主干是:

反问句：Consider whether it be not inconsistent and unjust to subjugate women?

陈述句：It is inconsistent and unjust to subjugate women.

(subjugate: 征服，使服从 to bring under control and governance as a subject)

让女性屈服于男性是不一致和不公平的。

整个句子理解:

思考一下，当男性为自己的自由斗争的时候，可以被允许为自己的幸福做判断的时候，即使你坚定地认为你是为了促进女性的幸福，让女性屈服难道不是前后矛盾和不公平的吗?

二、反问句练习

1. Is life so dear, or peace so sweet, as to be purchased at the price of chains and slavery?

2. Has it not, on the contrary, invariably been found that momentary passions, and immediate interests, have a more active and imperious control over human conduct than general or remote considerations of policy, utility, or justice?

3. Shall a government which has been thus strong and vigorous, be accused of imbecility, and abandoned for want of energy？

4. And is it not evident that the great conserving principle of Societies, which makes the division of powers a source of harmony, has been expressed and revealed by nature itself, when it divided the functions of the two sexes in so obviously distinct a manner?

5. Who made man the exclusive judge, if woman partake with him the gift of reason?

6. Must I argue that a system thus marked with blood and stained with pollution is wrong?

7. Fellow-citizens, pardon me, allow me to ask, why am I called upon to speak here to-day? What have I, or those I represent, to do with your national independence? Are the great principles of political freedom and of natural justice, embodied in that Declaration of Independence, extended to us? and am I, therefore, called upon to bring our humble offering to the national altar, and to confess the benefits and express devout gratitude for the blessings resulting from your independence to us?

三、反问句练习参考译文和理解

1. Is life so dear, or peace so sweet, as to be purchased at the price of chains and slavery?

生命是如此可贵，和平是如此甜美，以至于要付出枷锁和奴役的代价吗?

= 如果要付出枷锁和奴役的代价，那么生命就不可贵，和平也不是甜美的。

2. Has it not, on the contrary, invariably been found that momentary passions, and immediate interests, have a more active and imperious control over human conduct than general or remote considerations of policy, utility, or justice?

相反，难道我们不是总发现冲动的情感和当下的利益比整体和长远的政策、统一和正义的考虑会更加影响人的行为吗?

= 我们总是发现……

3. Shall a government which has been thus strong and vigorous, be accused of imbecility, and abandoned for want of energy ?

这样强大而有活力的政府难道应该被指控是无能的，然后因为缺乏能量而被抛弃吗?

= 这样的政府不应该被指控和抛弃。

4. And is it not evident that the great conserving principle of societies, which makes the division of powers a source of harmony, has been expressed and revealed by nature itself, when it divided the functions of the two sexes in so obviously distinct a manner?

维持社会的原则，让权力和谐地分工，让两性的功能明显地区分开来，是被自然自身所展现出来的。这难道不明显吗?

= 这很明显：当维持社会的原则并把两性的功能如此明显地区分开来的时候，这个原则是被自然本身所展现出来的。

5. Who made man the exclusive judge, if woman partake with him the gift of reason?

如果女性也和男性同样拥有理智，谁让男性成为唯一的决定者?

= 男性不应该是唯一的决定者，因为女性也是有理智的。

6. Must I argue that a system thus marked with blood and stained with pollution is wrong?

我需要去说这种带着血和肮脏的体系是错误的吗?

= 这种体系的错误是不言自明的，不需要任何人去说出来。

7. Fellow-citizens, pardon me, allow me to ask, why am I called upon to speak here today? What have I, or those I represent, to do with your national independence? Are the great principles of political freedom and of natural justice, embodied in that *Declaration of Independence*, extended to us? and am I, therefore, called upon to bring our humble offering to the national altar, and to confess the benefits and express devout gratitude for the blessings resulting from your independence to us?

这个段落全是反问句，这是一个黑人运动家道格拉斯在美国国庆节上的演讲，当时很多人都在庆祝美国独立。

段落的主要意思：我(道格拉斯)其实本来不应该来做演讲；我和我所代表的人和你们的(白人听众的)国家独立没有关系；在独立宣言中所体现的政治自由和天生的公正并没有赋予我们；所以我们不应该被召唤来庆祝这个节日，也不应该期待我们来表达虔诚的感激。

历史类文章句子障碍 3——否定句

英语中的否定句是比较复杂的，从形式上来说有以下几种。

第 *1* 种：全部否定。

第 *2* 种：部分否定。

第 *3* 种：双重否定。

第 *4* 种：表面否定实际肯定。

在讲解这些概念之前，先和大家梳理一下英语中表达肯定和否定的词汇。

- 全部肯定：both、all、every 家族 (everyone、everybody、everything、everywhere)、always、altogether、wholly、entirely 等。
- 部分肯定：some 家族 (someone、somebody、something、somewhere、sometimes)、either、certain (某些) 等。
- 全部否定：neither、none、no 家族 (nobody、nowhere、nothing)、never、not at all 等。

这些词单独使用可以表达全部肯定、部分肯定和全部否定的意义。比如：

1. All of my friends are pianists. 我的朋友们都是钢琴家。
2. Some of my friends are pianists. 我的朋友们有的是钢琴家，有的不是钢琴家。
3. None of my friends are pianists. 我的朋友中没有钢琴家。

但是如果这些词混合在一起使用，那么意思就可能很难理解，或者通常被错误理解。比如：

All my friends are not pianists.

Not all my friends are pianists.

My friend Edward are nobody but a pianist.

Some of my friends are not pianists.

Edward can never be a more well-known pianist.

大家可以先思考一下这些句子的意思。待会看完本部分内容之后再回来思考这些句子的真正意思。

这种肯定、否定的考查在 SAT 中曾经出现过，下面给大家看这个试题。

To create its special herd of goats, GTC used microinjection, the same technique that produced GloFish and AquAdvantage salmon. The company's scientists took the gene for human antithrombin and injected it directly into fertilized goat eggs. Then they implanted the eggs in the wombs of female goats. When the kids were born, some of them proved to be transgenic, the human gene nestled safely in their cells. The researchers paired the antithrombin gene with a promoter (which is a sequence of DNA that controls gene activity) that is normally active in the goat's mammary glands during milk production. When the transgenic females lactated, the promoter turned the transgene on and the goats' udders filled with milk containing antithrombin. All that was left to do was to collect the milk, and extract and purify the protein.

Which of the following does the author suggest about the "female goats"?

A) They secreted antithrombin in their milk after giving birth.

B) Some of their kids were not born with the antithrombin gene.

C) They were the first animals to receive microinjections.

D) Their cells already contained genes usually found in humans

【解析】这道题实际上不难，但考生还是很容易选错的。大部分考生会选择 A 选项或者 D 选项，原因在于没看清题目和选项的 they/their 指代。题目问的是 female goats，所以选项中 they/their 都是指代 female goats. 而很多考生看到原文 "When the kids were born, some of them proved to be transgenic, the human gene nestled safely in their cells." 就误以为选项代词指的是 kids，所以选择了 A 或 D。

大部分考生没有选择 B，认为这个选项中的 "were not born with the antithrombin gene" 和原文相反。但是文章中说 some of them proved to be transgenic，言外之意就是 some of them proved not to be transgenic，本质上是一样的，都是部分肯定或者部分否定。

所以答案选 B。

一、全部否定

1. 全部否定词 + 肯定谓语词

Nobody survived. 没人存活。

2. 全部肯定词 + 否定谓语词

All died. 全部死亡了。

All his words were incredible. 他的话都不可信。

（注意和 All his words were not credible "他的话不是都能相信" 的区别）

3. 否定词 + 不定代词

He could not remember anything. 他什么也不记得。

He did not see anybody. 他没有见任何人。

二、部分否定

1. 部分肯定 = 部分否定

Some kids are present.

= Some kids are not present.

= Some kids are absent.

2. 对全部否定或者全部肯定的否定。（这句话有点绕）

全部否定：All died.

在此基础上否定：Not all died.（部分死亡，部分没死）

全部肯定：All that glisters is gold.

在此基础上否定：Not all that glisters is gold.（闪光的东西未必都是黄金）

简而言之：

all...not... = not all = some

everybody... not... = not everybody = somebody

always...not... = not always = sometimes

三、双重否定

1. 委婉语：否定词 + 否定谓语词

He is not incapable.

他并非无能。（其实表达的是他还是有些能力的）

She was not indifferent to her children.

她对自己孩子不是冷漠的。(其实表达她对孩子比较关心)

2. 强调作用：否定词 + 否定词

There is no right to speak without investigation.

没有调查就没有发言权。

I will never go there without you.

没有你我绝不会去那儿。(只有你去我才去)

3. 强调作用：否定词 + but

I have nothing but money. (钱我有的是)

I want nobody but you. (我只要你)

四、表面否定实际肯定

否定词 + too/over/more

You cannot be too careful when driving. (开车时候一定要小心)

We can never emphasize that too much. (再强调也不为过 = 一定要多强调)

I could not agree more. (完全同意)

五、官方试题典型例句分析

1. It may readily be conceived, that by thus attempting to make one sex equal to the other, both are degraded; and from so preposterous a medley of the works of nature nothing could ever result but weak men and disorderly women.

【解析】第一句中 both are degraded 是全部否定。如果性别完全平等的话，那么两者都会被降级。

第二句中存在 nothing 这个否定词和 but，所以是双重否定，意思是只会产生柔弱的男人和骚动的女性。此外，这句话的语序大家要注意，正常语序是：

Nothing but weak men and disorderly women could ever result from so preposterous a medley of the works of nature.

2. How does it become a man to behave toward this American government today? I answer, that he cannot without disgrace be associated with it.

【解析】整个是设问句(自问自答)。回答部分存在两个否定词 not 和 without，构成双重否定。说的是如果一个人和美国政府有关联就一定是不光彩的。

3. In neither case, is the interposition of mob law, either necessary, justifiable, or excusable.

【解析】本句明显是一个全部否定，neither 意为“两者都不”，句子意思是不管在这两种情况下的任何一种，暴民法（私刑）都不是必要的、合理的和可以原谅的。

4. The extensive cultivation of cotton can perhaps hardly be expected, but from the previous establishment of domestic manufactories of the article; and the surest encouragement and vent, for the others, would result from similar establishments in respect to them.

Alexander Hamilton, “Report on Manufactures”

【解析】句子中的 hardly（否定副词）和 but 构成双重否定。

棉花的广泛种植是不能预期的，除非事先建立这个物品的国内制造业。（注意这里的 article 意思为“物品”，文中指的是 cotton。句子强调只有事先建立制造业才能有农作物的广泛种植）

5. I am conscious that an equal division of property is impracticable. But the consequences of this enormous inequality producing so much misery to the bulk of mankind, legislators cannot invent too many devices for subdividing property.

【解析】第一句：我意识到财产的平均分配是不切实际的。

第二句以 but 开头，说明和第一句形成转折或对比关系。其主句是“legislators cannot invent too many devices for subdividing property”，如果理解为立法者不能创造很多方法进行财产分配，那么明显和第一句无法形成转折逻辑。所以这句话是表面否定实际肯定：立法者应当创造出很多的方法进行财产分配（立法者创造的方法再多也不为过）。

历史类文章句子障碍 4——熟词僻义

所谓的熟词僻义，指的是单词可能大家比较熟悉，但是在特定的语境中是别的含义，而这个含义又不是特别常见。比如 article 这个单词，最常见的意思是“文章”，比较少见的意思是“法案”，但是还可以表示“物品”；比如 passage 通常表示“文章”，但是如果是“I wonder why some senators object to the passage of the Constitution”，这里面的 passage 则表示“通过，赞同”，来自动词 pass。

这里给大家汇总一下 SAT 中最为重要的熟词僻义单词。

1. subject

常见意思是“主题，科目，话题”，还可以表示：

(1) 实验对象 (an individual whose reactions or responses are studied)

Using functional magnetic resonance imaging (fMRI), these researchers recorded the brain activity of SCRABBLE players and control **subjects**.

The **subjects** for this investigation were selected randomly

(2) 被统治者，臣民 (one that is placed under authority or control)

A monarch has a duty to his **subjects**.

I think we should be men first, and **subjects** afterward.

(3) 受影响，使屈服，使承受 (to bring under control or dominion，to cause or force to undergo or endure)

It is unfair for men to subject women.

Men being, as has been said, by nature, all free, equal, and independent, no one can be put out of this estate, and **subjected** to the political power of another, without his own consent.

(4) 此外还要注意，这个单词变成形容词 subjective，表示“主观的”

Subjective things depend on your own ideas and opinions: there isn't any universal truth. Subjective is the opposite of objective.

2. observe

常见意思是“观察”，还可以表示：

(1) 遵守 (follow)

But I do mean to say, that, although bad laws, if they exist, should be repealed as soon as possible, still while they continue in force, for the sake of example, they should be religiously **observed**.

(2) 提及，发现，评论，庆祝 (mention、discover、celebrate)

The news reports that the group **observed** a moment of silence for all those killed by gun violence.

She **observed** that his presentation took up too much time.

3. institution

通常表示“机构，组织”，还可以是：

传统，习俗 (a custom that for a long time has been an important feature of some group or society)

Our life-philosophy, molds our inherited political **institutions**, and reforms the oldest and toughest customs, like marriage and property.

4. cause

通常作动词，表示“导致”，还可以是：

(1) 原因 (events that provide the generative force that is the origin of something)

We must reduce our release of carbon dioxide, the heat-absorbing gas that is the principal **cause** of global warming.

(2) 行为，事业 (something worth fighting for, a series of actions advancing a principle or tending toward a particular end)

Under ordinary circumstances, I even like your obstinate braying and your mulish devotion to the **cause**.

5. object

通常表示“客体，物体”，也可以表示：

(1) 反对 (express or raise an objection or protest or criticism or express dissent)

She never **objected** to the amount of work her boss charged her with.

When asked to drive the truck, she objected that she did not have a driver’s license

(2) 目标 (objective, goal)

The sole object of her trip was to see her children.

(3) 此外需要注意，object 作动词表示“反对”，变成名词是 objection；而 objective 作名词表示“目标”，作形容词表示“客观的”。

The House criminal justice committee agreed to the proposal without **objection** Wednesday, sending it to the full House for debate.

“Our **objective** is not a technological revolution,” she says, “but a cultural one that is able to put the citizen at the heart of society.”

6. ground

常见意思是“地板，地面”，还可以表示：

(1) 基于，根据，依靠 (base，use as a basis for; found on)

His conclusions are **grounded** on long-time observation.

(2) 另外，在 SAT 选项中会出现 groundless 这个词，意思是“无根据的，无理由的”

He dismissed Washington’s concerns that its products pose security threats as “**groundless** suspicions”.

7. faculty

常见意思是“教员，员工”，其实更多时候可以表示：

能力，才能 (an inherent capability, power, or function)

One may have great **faculties** of memory, sight, mobility, charm, math, and musicality, but, as Beethoven was in the end, might be robbed of the **faculty** of hearing.

Each individual will prove his or her capacities, in the only way in which capacities can be proved—by trial; and the world will have the benefit of the best **faculties** of all its inhabitants.

8. interest

通常意思是“兴趣，吸引”，还可以表示：

(1) 关心，利益 (a sense of concern with, benefit)

It seems to us incontestable that our common happiness, above all that of women, requires that they never aspire to the exercise of political rights and functions. Here we must seek their interests in the wishes of nature.

(2) 股份 (right, title, or legal share in something)

If you have an interest in a company, it means you own part of it.

9. charge

通常表示“充电，收费”，还可以表示：

(1) 责任，义务 (duty, responsibility or obligation to)

She was charged with supervising the creation of a concordance.

His charge was deliver a message.

(2) 指责，指控 (blame for, make a claim of wrongdoing or misbehavior against)

She is charged with shoplifting from grocery store on Christmas Eve.

The five men are charged with assisting in illegal border crossing and may be jailed up to 10 years.

(3) 此外，这个单词还有“掌管，控制”等意思。

10. address

通常表示“地址”，还可以表示：

(1) 演讲，作演讲 (the act of delivering a formal spoken communication to an audience， give a speech)

Gettysburg Address is a three-minute address by Abraham Lincoln during the American Civil War at the dedication of a national cemetery on the site of the Battle of Gettysburg.

(2) 处理 (to deal with)

Regardless, business experts believe that economic inequities must be addressed.

11. compelling

(1) 有力的 (powerful,strong)

Gary Dickey, a Democrat who served as former Gov. Tom Vilsack's general counsel, said the abrupt termination suggests that Reynolds was presented with compelling evidence of wrongdoing.

(2) 有说服力的，引人注目的 (tending to persuade by forcefulness of argument)

Mr. McMahon is among the most compelling of the many analysts who conclude that that country's economic miracle will end painfully.

12. bear

常见意思是“熊，忍受”，还可以表示：

(1) 养育，生育 (give birth to)，其实 born 这个词的原形就是 bear

Rising slowly from the earth that bore me and gave me sustenance, I am carried helplessly toward an uninhabited and hostile, or at best indifferent, part of the earth, littered with the bones of explorers and the wrecks of ships.

(2) 携带，承担 (carry，undertake)

The wind is still from the south, bearing us steadily northward at the speed of a trotting dog.

The right to keep and bear arms shall not be infringed.

13. constitution

(1) 首字母大写表示“宪法”。US Constitution

(2) 法律，传统 (an established law or custom)

(3) 构造 (the physical makeup of the individual especially with respect to the health, strength, and appearance of the body)

14. want

(1) 缺乏，需求 (the state of needing something that is absent or unavailable)

The want of proper books is a serious concern.

(2) 贫困 (a state of extreme poverty)

15. 其他常见词汇总

reflection = thought

contain = check = control

tear = split

compromise = damage

sound = healthy, valid

conviction = belief

qualify = limit

disposed = willing

yield = submit = surrender

历史类文章句子障碍 5——语序

历史类文章中会出现常见的倒装结构，比如：

1. 句首是否定词或否定短语

No sooner did he see the old prejudice wearing away than he immediately began sowing the seeds of a new inveteracy, as if he were afraid that England and France would cease to be enemies.

【解析】no sooner...than... 结构。他一看到陈旧的偏见正在消失的时候就开始散播新的偏见的种子，好像他很担心英法两国会停止成为敌人。

In no sense do I advocate evading or defying the law, as would the rabid segregationists.

【解析】in no sense 开头的倒装句式，正常语序是：I, in no sense, advocate... 我并不是宣扬像那些激进的种族隔离者一样逃避或是挑衅法律。

2. 虚拟语气省略 if 倒装

Could one of these Sequoia Kings come to town in all its godlike majesty so as to be strikingly seen and allowed to plead its own cause, there would never again be any lack of defenders.

【解析】整个句子是虚拟语气，前面省略 if，可还原成：If one of these Sequoia Kings could come to town... 如果这些红杉树能够来到城镇让大家看到而且请求自己的事情，那么就不会缺少保护者了。

3. 表语置于句首

Close at hand is a bridge over the River Thames, and admirable vantage ground for us to make a survey.

【解析】正常语序是 A bridge over the River Thames is close at hand, ...

In proportion to the strength of a feeling is the tenacity with which it clings to the forms and circumstances with which it has even accidentally become associated.

【解析】正常语序是： The tenacity (with which…) is in proportion to the strength of a feeling. 这种保持力是和情感成正比的。

4. 为了强调或是避免“头重脚轻”而进行语序变换

Guard with jealous attention the public liberty.

【解析】这句话是个祈使句，呼吁大家保护公众自由。这句话的主干是 Guard...the public liberty，介词短语 with jealous attention 正常应该放在最后，这里放在中间是为了强调。另外，这里的 jealous 根据语境理解应该是正面的，不能理解为“嫉妒的”，而是“仔细的，小心翼翼的”。整个句子的意思是“我们必须小心翼翼地保护公众自由”。

The Americans have applied to the sexes the great principle of political economy which governs the manufactures of our age, by carefully dividing the duties of man from those of woman, in order that the great work of society may be the better carried on.

【解析】整个句子意思是 apply A to B（把 A 运用到 B）；但是因为 A 的成分在句子中又连接了定语从句，导致成分过多，所以后置。正常语序为：

The Americans have applied the great principle of…to the sexes. 美国人把这样一个伟大的原则运用到性别上。

整篇文章理解训练

逐句分析这篇文章，分析长难句、其他典型句型和单词用法（反问、否定句、熟词僻义等）。

Give Me Liberty or Give Me Death

Patrick Henry, March 23, 1775

No man thinks more highly than I do of the patriotism, as well as abilities, of the very worthy gentlemen who have just addressed the House. But different men often see the same subject in different lights; and, therefore, I hope it will not be thought disrespectful to those gentlemen if, entertaining as I do opinions of a character very opposite to theirs, I shall speak forth my sentiments freely and without reserve. This is no time for ceremony. The questing before the House is one of awful moment to this country. For my own part, I consider it as nothing less than a question of freedom or slavery; and in proportion to the magnitude of the subject ought to be the freedom of the debate. It is only in this way that we can hope to arrive at truth, and fulfill the great responsibility which we hold to God and our country. Should I keep back my opinions at such a time, through fear of giving offense, I should consider myself as guilty of treason towards my country, and of an act of disloyalty toward the Majesty of Heaven, which I revere above all earthly kings.

Mr. President, it is natural to man to indulge in the illusions of hope. We are apt to shut our eyes against a painful truth, and listen to the song of that siren till she transforms us into beasts. Is this the part of wise men, engaged in a great and arduous struggle for liberty? Are we disposed to be of the number of those who, having eyes, see not, and, having ears, hear not, the things which so nearly concern their temporal salvation? For my part, whatever anguish of spirit it may cost, I am willing to know the whole truth; to know the worst, and to provide for it.

I have but one lamp by which my feet are guided, and that is the lamp of experience. I know of no way of judging of the future but by the past. And judging by the past, I wish to know what there has been in the conduct of the British ministry for the last ten years to justify those hopes with which gentlemen have been pleased to solace themselves and the House. Is it that insidious smile with which our petition has been lately received? Trust it not, sir; it will prove a snare to your feet. Suffer not yourselves to be betrayed with a kiss. Ask yourselves how this gracious reception of our petition comports with those warlike preparations which cover our waters and darken our land. Are fleets and armies necessary to a work of love and reconciliation? Have we shown ourselves so unwilling to be reconciled that force must be called in to win back our love? Let us not deceive ourselves, sir. These are the implements of war and subjugation; the last arguments to which kings resort. I ask gentlemen, sir, what means this martial array, if its purpose be not to force us to submission? Can gentlemen assign any other possible motive for it? Has Great Britain any enemy, in this quarter of the world, to call for all this accumulation of navies and armies? No, sir, she has none. They are meant for us: they can be meant for no other. They are sent over to bind and rivet upon us those chains which the British ministry have been so long forging. And what have we to oppose to them? Shall we try argument? Sir, we have been trying that for the last ten years. Have we anything new to offer upon the subject? Nothing. We have held the subject up in every light of which it is capable; but it has been all in vain. Shall we resort to entreaty and humble supplication? What terms shall we find which have not been already exhausted? Let us not, I beseech you, sir, deceive ourselves. Sir, we have done everything that could be done to avert the storm which is now coming on. We have petitioned; we have remonstrated; we have supplicated; we have prostrated ourselves before the throne, and have implored its interposition to arrest the tyrannical hands of the ministry and Parliament. Our petitions have been slighted; our remonstrances have produced additional violence and insult; our supplications have been disregarded; and we have been spurned, with contempt, from the foot of the throne! In vain, after these things, may we indulge the fond hope of peace and reconciliation. There is no longer any room for hope.

If we wish to be free—if we mean to preserve inviolate those inestimable privileges for which we have been so long contending—if we mean not basely to abandon the noble struggle in which we have been so long engaged, and which we have pledged ourselves never to abandon until the glorious object of our contest shall be obtained—we must fight!

……

【参考译文】

我比任何人更钦佩刚刚在议会上发言的先生们的爱国精神和才能。但是，对同一事物的看法往往因人而异。因此，尽管我的观点与他们截然不同，我还是要毫无保留地、自由地予以阐述，并且希望不要因此而被视作对先生们的不敬。现在不是讲客气的时候。摆在议会代表们面前的问题关系到国家的存亡。我认为，这是关系到享受自由还是蒙受奴役的大问题，而且正由于它事关重大，我们的辩论就必须做到各抒己见。只有这样，我们才有可能弄清事实真相，才能不辜负上帝和祖国赋予我们的重任。在这种时刻，如果怕冒犯别人而闭口不言，我认为就是叛国，就是对比世间所有国君更为神圣的上帝的不忠。

议长先生，对希望抱有幻觉是人的天性。我们易于闭起眼睛不愿正视痛苦的现实，并倾听海妖惑人的歌声，让她把我们化作禽兽。在为自由而进行艰苦卓绝的斗争中，这难道是有理智的人的作为吗？难道我们愿意成为对获得自由这样休戚相关的事视而不见、充耳不闻的人吗？就我来说，无论在精神上有多么痛苦，我仍然愿意了解全部事实真相和最坏的事态，并为之做好充分准备。

我只有一盏指路明灯，那就是经验之灯。除了过去的经验，我没有什么别的方法可以判断未来。而依据过去的经验，我倒希望知道，10 年来英国政府的所作所为，凭什么足以使各位先生有理由满怀希望，并欣然用来安慰自己和议会？难道就是最近接受我们请愿时的那种狡诈的微笑吗？不要相信这种微笑，先生们，事实已经证明它是你们脚边的陷阱。不要被人家的亲吻出卖吧！请你们自问，接受我们请愿时的和气亲善和遍布我们海陆疆域的大规模备战如何能够相称？难道出于对我们的爱护与和解，有必要动用战舰和军队吗？难道我们流露过决不和解的愿望，以至为了赢回我们的爱，而必须诉诸武力吗？我们不要再欺骗自己了，先生们。这些都是战争和征服的工具，是国王采取的最后论辩手段。我要请问先生们，这些战争部署如果不是为了迫使我们就范，那又意味着什么？哪位先生能够指出有其他动机？难道在世界的这一角，还有别的敌人值得大不列颠如此兴师动众，集结起庞大的海陆武装吗？不，先生们，没有任何敌人了。一切都是针对我们的，而不是别人。他们是派来给我们套紧那条由英国政府长期以来铸造的锁链的。我们应该如何进行抵抗呢？还靠辩论吗？先生们，我们已经辩论了10年了。难道还有什么新的御敌之策吗？没有了。我们已经从各方面经过了考虑，但一切都是枉然。难道我们还要苦苦哀告、卑词乞求吗？难道我们还有什么更好的策略没有使用过吗？先生们，我请求你们，千万不要再自欺欺人了。为了阻止这场即将来临的风暴，一切该做的都已经做了。我们请愿过，我们抗议过，我们哀求过；我们曾拜倒在英王御座前，恳求他制止国会和内阁的残暴行径。可是，我们的请愿受到蔑视，我们的抗议反而招致更多的暴力和侮辱，我们的哀求被置之不理，我们被轻蔑地从御座边一脚踢开了。事到如今，我们怎么还能沉迷于虚无缥缈的和平希望之中呢？没有任何希望的余地了。

假如我们想获得自由，并维护我们长期以来为之献身的崇高权利，假如我们不愿彻底放弃多年来的斗争，不获全胜，决不收兵。那么，我们就必须战斗！

历史类文章段落的典型结构

1. 观点＋例证

But, on the other hand, the delay of this Declaration to this time has many great advantages attending it. The hopes of reconciliation, which were fondly entertained by multitudes of honest and well meaning, though weak and mistaken people, have been gradually and, at last, totally extinguished. Time has been given for the whole people maturely to consider the great question of independence, and to ripen their judgment, dissipate their fears, and allure their hopes, by discussing it in newspapers and pamphlets, by debating it in assemblies, conventions, Committees of safety and inspection, in town and country meetings, as well as in private conversations, so that the whole people, in every colony of the thirteen, have now adopted it as their own act. This will cement the union, and avoid those heats, and perhaps convulsions, which might have been occasioned by such a Declaration, six months ago.	首先第一句直接说明观点，延缓独立宣言是有很多好处的。 后续是具体描述，打消大家期待和解的幻想；时间让大家想法更加成熟，驱散恐惧。

2. 观点排比

Let every American, every lover of liberty, every well wisher to his posterity, swear by the blood of the Revolution, **never** to violate in the least particular,the laws of the country; and **never** to tolerate their violation by others. As the patriots of seventy-six did to the support of *the Declaration of Independence*, so to the support of the Constitution and Laws, **let** every American pledge his life, his property, and his sacred honor;—**let** every man remember that to violate the law, is to trample on the blood of his father, and to tear the character of his own, and his children's liberty. **Let** reverence for the laws, be breathed by every American mother, to the lisping babe, that prattles on her lap—**let** it be taught in schools, inseminaries, and in colleges;—**let** it be written in Primers, spelling books, and in Almanacs; —**let** it be preached from the pulpit, proclaimed in legislative halls, and enforced in courts of justice. And, in short, **let** it become the political religion of the nation; and let the old and the young, the rich and the poor, the grave and the gay, of all sexes and tongues, and colors and conditions, sacrifice unceasingly upon its altars…	这样排比的段落在阅读时是非常简单的：理解第一句就可以理解后面所有句子的意思和作用。从第一句得知作者的主要观点就是每个人都应该遵守法律，而且不要容忍别人违反法律。 看到这种段落大家可提速阅读，迅速找到下一个排比地方，直到排比结束。

All this is true. Yet in the history and in the present state of our Indian Empire I see ample reason for exultation and for a good hope. I see that we have established order where we found confusion. I see that the petty dynasties...which, a century ago, kept all India in constant agitation, have been quelled by one overwhelming power. I see that the predatory tribes, which, in the middle of the last century, passed annually over the harvests of India with the destructive rapidity of a hurricane, have.been. extirpated by the English sword, or compelled to exchange the pursuits of rapine for those of industry.	这里一共三个段落，其中第一段开头出现了让步和转折，转折后作者指出看到很多值得高兴的事和充满希望的原因。 第二段和第三段中有很多排比句，所以在阅读时候可以提速，不会影响对主要观点和结构的把握。

I look back for many years, and I see scarcely a trace of the vices which blemished the splendid fame of the first conquerors of Bengal. I see peace studiously preserved. I see faith inviolably maintained towards feeble and dependent states. I see confidence gradually infused into the minds of suspicious neighbors. I see the horrors of war mitigated by the chivalrous and Christian spirit of Europe. I see examples of moderation and clemency, such as I should seek in vain in the annals of any other victorious and dominant nation...	

3. 让步+观点

I am conscious that an equal division of property is impracticable. But the consequences of this enormous inequality producing so much misery to the bulk of mankind, legislators cannot invent too many devices for subdividing property, only taking care to let their subdivisions go hand in hand with the natural affections of the human mind. The descent of property of every kind therefore to all the children, or to all the brothers and sisters, or other relations in equal degree is a politic measure, and a practicable one Another means of silently lessening the inequality of property is to exempt all from taxation below a certain point, and to tax the higher portions of property in geometrical progression as they rise. Whenever there is in any country, uncultivated lands and unemployed poor, it is clear that the laws of property have been so far extended as to violate natural right. The earth is given as a common stock for man to labour and live on. If, for the encouragement of industry we allow it to be appropriated, we must take care that other employment be furnished to those excluded from the appropriation...	第一句先让步，作者意识到财产的完全平均分配是不切实际的。让步之后立即转折，但是立法者应该创造更多的方法去分配财产。 后续通过举例来说明有哪些方法可以采用，从而使财产分配更加公平。 (1) 亲戚间的分配。 (2) 税收政策。

4. 对方观点＋反驳

When anyone asserts that the class of skilled and unskilled manual laborers of the United States is worse of now in respect to diet, clothing, lodgings, furniture, fuel, and lights; in respect to the age at which they can marry; the number of children they can provide for; the start in life which they can give to their children, and their chances of accumulating capital, than they ever have been at any former time, **he makes a reckless assertion for which no facts have been oferred in proof**. Upon an appeal to facts, the contrary of this assertion would be clearly established. It suffices, therefore, to challenge those who are responsible for the assertion to make it good.	开头先说对方的观点，一些人提出了很多观点：工人阶级生活状况日益恶化：在结婚年龄、抚养孩子数量、给孩子的生活起点、积累资本的机会等方面都变得更加糟糕。 进行反驳，说明这种说法是毫无根据的。

There are people in Europe who, confounding together the different characteristics of the sexes, would make of man and woman beings not only equal but alike. They would give to both the same functions, impose on both the same duties, and grant to both the same rights; they would mix them in all things—their occupations, their pleasures, their business. **It may readily be conceived, that by thus attempting to make one sex equal to the other, both are degraded**; and from so preposterous a medley of the works of nature nothing could ever result but weak men and disorderly women.	对方观点（欧洲的某些人）：混淆性别的不同特征，认为男性和女性不仅平等而且相似，赋予两者相同的作用、相同的义务和相同的权利。 反驳，这样做的话，两者都被贬低了（负面后果）。

5. 现象＋评论

That half the human race is excluded by the other half from any participation in government, that they are native by birth but foreign by law in the very land where they were born; and that they are property-owners yet have no direct influence or representation: are all political phenomena apparently impossible to explain on abstract	首先描述了社会现状：女性不能参与政府，不受法律保护，是财产的所有者却不能直接处置财产。

principle. But on another level of ideas, the question changes and may be easily resolved. The purpose of all these institutions must be the happiness of the greatest number. Everything that leads us farther from this purpose is in error; everything that brings us closer is truth. If the exclusion from public employments decreed against women leads to a greater sum of mutual happiness for the two sexes, then this becomes a law that all Societies have been compelled to acknowledge and sanction.	再评论：制定这些制度的目的是为了最多数人的幸福。只要是有利于大家的幸福就是正确的，就应该得到社会的认可。

6. 回应型段落

In complaining of what I said in my speech at Springfield, in which he says I accepted my nomination for the Senatorship…he again quotes that portion in which I said that "a house divided against itself cannot stand." **Let me say a word in regard to that matter.** He tries to persuade us that there must be a variety in the different institutions of the States of the Union; that that variety necessarily proceeds from the variety of soil, climate, of the face of the country, and the difference in the natural features of the States. I agree to all that. Have these very matters ever produced any difficulty among us? Not at all. Have we ever had any quarrel over the fact that they have laws in Louisiana designed to regulate the commerce that springs from the production of sugar? Or because we have a different class relative to the production of flour in this State? Have they produced any differences? Not at all. They are the very cements of this Union. They don't make the house a "house divided against itself." They are the props that hold up the house and sustain the Union.	Let me say a word… 很明显是回应第一篇文章作者。 对于第一篇文章中作者认为每个州是不一样的，所以应该有不一样的制度，作者是认同的(I agree to all that) 后面用反问的方式强调这些问题没有导致任何困难和冲突。 * 对于回应型段落要重点看作者的回应是什么，是正面还是负面态度。

Before I proceed to make some additions to the reasons which have been adduced by my honorable friend over the way, I must take the liberty to **make some observations on what was said by another gentleman**, (Mr. Henry). He told us that this Constitution ought to be rejected because it endangered the public liberty, in his opinion, in many instances. Give me leave to make one answer to that observation: Let the dangers which this system is supposed to be replete with be clearly pointed out: if any dangerous and unnecessary powers be given to the general legislature, let them be plainly demonstrated; and let us not rest satisfied with general assertions of danger, without examination.	段落开头make some observation on what was said by another gentleman（指第一篇文章作者）。说明还是先回应：他告诉我们宪法应该被否定，因为宪法破坏了公众自由。 回应：let the dangers be clearly pointed out; let them be plainly demonstrated. 言外之意就是第一篇文章的作者没有清晰地指出宪法有什么危险，没有实质性证据。

第九章

双篇对比文章与题型

SAT SAT SAT SAT SAT SAT SAT SAT SAT SAT SAT SAT SAT SAT SAT SAT SAT

阅读中其中一篇是由 Passage 1 和 Passage 2 构成。每篇文章差不多有 40—50 行，所以整体长度和其他四篇类似。双篇文章的题目也是 10—11 题，通常前四题是有关 Passage 1 的，中间四题是有关 Passage 2 的，最后几题与两篇文章都相关。我们重点讨论有关两篇文章的题目。

题型识别

1. 求同题

比如要求考生找出两篇文章的共同话题、共同观点、共同细节。题干形式如下：

- The main purpose of both passages (each passage) is to…
- Based on the passages, both authors would most likely agree that…
- The authors of both passages would most likely agree with which of the following statements about…
- One central idea in both passages is that…

2. 求异题

比如问考生两篇文章的不同观点、不同细节、不同写作手法，甚至是不同的语气。题干形式如下：

- How do...and...differ in their discussion of...
- Unlike the author of passage 1/2, the author of passage 2/1 believes/states that…
- Unlike the author of passage 1/2, the author of passage 2/1 makes extensive use of…
- Unlike that of passage 1/2, the tone of passage 2/1 is more…

3. 文章关系题

考查考生对两篇文章的主要观点的把握并判断主要观点的关系（观点一直、观点相反、观点交叉）。题干形式如下：

- Which choice best states the relationship between the two passages?
- Which choice best describes the ways that the two authors conceive of…
- Which choice identifies a central tension between the two passages?

4. 回应题

这种题目主要问某篇文章的作者如何回应另外一篇文章的某些单词 / 短语 / 句子 / 观点。题干形式如下：

- How would the author of passage 1/2 most likely respond to…in lines…of passage 2/1?
- Which choice best describes how the author of passage1/2 most likely have reacted to…in lines… of passage 2/1?
- Based on the passages, …would most likely describe…as…

双篇文章的关系分类

双篇文章的话题一定是一致的，不然不会放在一起进行讨论。而对于同一个话题，其观点基本上可以分成三种：观点一致、观点冲突、观点交叉。下面我们逐一举例进行分析。

1. 观点一致

观点一致的两篇文章在讨论一个话题的时候，一般来说观点一致、相互支持；或者某篇抽象，另外一篇给出具体信息；或者某篇给出另外一篇的背景。

Passage 1

Food has always been considered one of the most salient markers of cultural traditions. When I was a small child, food was the only thing that helped identify my family as Filipino American. We ate Filipino food and my father put salty fish sauce on everything. However, even this connection lessened as I grew older. As my parents became more adapted, we ate less typically Filipino food. When I was twelve, my mother took cooking classes and learned to make French and Italian dishes. When I was in high school, we ate chicken marsala and shrimp fra diablo more often than Filipino dishes like pansit lug-lug.

Passage 2

Jean Anthelme Brillat—who in 1825 confidently announced, "Tell me what you eat, and I will tell you who you are" —would have no trouble describing cultural identities of the United States. Our food reveals us as tolerant adventurers who do not feel constrained by tradition. We "play with our food" far more readily than we preserve the culinary rules of our varied ancestors. American have no single national cuisine. What unites American eater culturally is how we eat, not what we eat. As eaters, Americans mingle the culinary traditions of many regions and cultures.

【Question】

Which choice best states the relationship between the two passages?

A) Passage 1 notes some problems for which passage 2 proposes solutions.

B) Passage 1 present ideas that are criticized by passage 2.

C) Passage 2 provides a larger context for the experiences described in passage 1.

D) Passage 2 provides an update of the situation described in passage 1.

【解析】第一篇文章主要是通过自身经历来描述其家庭饮食习惯的改变，小时候的食物只是菲律宾传统食品，后来开始尝试不同的饮食，比如法式食品或意式食品等。整篇文章表达的观点是食物是文化的重要标志，作为美国人，作者一家的饮食越来越多样化。

第二篇文章主要引用专家的观点进行阐述，文化是身份的标志，之后提到美国的饮食是多元化的。

所以，两篇文章的话题和观点一致。答案选择 C——第二篇文章为第一篇文章描述的经历提供了更广阔的背景。因为第二篇文章是站在整个国家的角度阐述的，而第一篇是基于个人经历，所以第二篇文章的背景更广阔。

但是，两篇文章也有不同的地方。比如在写作手法上，第一篇文章用 personal anecdote, 而第二篇文章用了 direct quotation.

2. 观点冲突

观点冲突的两篇文章是指一篇文章质疑 (question)、反对 (oppose)、挑战 (challenge) 或批判 (criticize) 另外一篇文章。

Passage 1

The first three years of life appear to be a crucial starting-point, a period particularly sensitive to the protective mechanisms of parental and family support. For millennia, parents have recognized the newborn's basic need for safety, nourishment, warmth, and nurturing. Now science has added stunning revelations about human development from birth to age three, confirming that parents and other adult caregivers play a critical role in influencing a child's development. No other period of human life is suited to learning as are a child's first three years. Babies raised by caring, attentive adults in safe, predictable environments are better learners than those raised with less attention in less secure settings.

Passage 2

Much early childhood literature suggests that the first three years of life are the critical years for brain development. Yet new findings in neuroscience suggest that the brain retains its ability to recognize itself in response to experience or injury throughout life: after the loss of sensory input from an amputated limb, for example, adults are able to learn new motor skills effectively. It may be useful to question the simplistic view that the brain becomes unbendable and increasingly difficult to modify beyond the first few years of life. If so, we should also be wary of claims that parents have only a single opportunity to help their children build better brains.

【Question】

Which choice best states the relationship between the two passages?

A) Passage 2 questions the assumption underlying the ideas expressed in passage 1.

B) Passage 2 mock those who support the argument presented in passage 1.

C) Passage 2 provides additional support for the ideas in passage 1.

D) Passage 2 urges changes as a result of the findings in passage 1.

【解析】第一篇文章的主要观点是生命的前三年是至关重要的，对小孩以后各方面的发展影响非常大。

第二篇文章的主要观点是大脑能够从伤害中恢复，能够自我调节和修复，也就是说，生命中任何时间段都可以帮助大脑提升能力。所以我们应该警惕那种认为父母只有一次机会帮助孩子发育大脑的说法。

因此，两篇文章主要观点相反，答案选择 A。

3. 观点交叉

观点交叉是指对于某个话题，两篇文章的主要观点既有一致的地方也有冲突的地方。

Questions 38–47 are based on the following passages.

Passage 1 is adapted from Stewart Brand, “The Case for Reviving Extinct Species.” ©2013 by *the National Geographic Society*. Passage 2 is adapted from the editors at Scientific American, “Why Efforts to Bring Extinct Species Back from the Dead Miss the Point.” ©2013 by Nature America, Inc.

Passage 1

Many extinct species—from the passenger pigeon to the woolly mammoth—might now be reclassified as “bodily, but not genetically, extinct.” They’re dead, but their DNA is recoverable from museum specimens and fossils, even those up to 200,000 years old.

Thanks to new developments in genetic technology, that DNA may eventually bring the animals back to life. Only species whose DNA is too old to be recovered, such as dinosaurs, are the ones to consider totally extinct, bodily and genetically.

But why bring vanished creatures back to life? It will be expensive and difficult. It will take decades. It won't always succeed. Why even try?

Why do we take enormous trouble to protect endangered species? The same reasons will apply to species brought back from extinction: to preserve biodiversity, to restore diminished ecosystems, to advance the science of preventing extinctions, and to undo harm that humans have caused in the past.

Furthermore, the prospect of de-extinction is profound news. That something as irreversible and final as extinction might be reversed is a stunning realization. The imagination soars. Just the thought of mammoths and passenger pigeons alive again invokes the awe and wonder that drives all conservation at its deepest level.

Passage 2

The idea of bringing back extinct species holds obvious gee-whiz appeal and a respite from a steady stream of grim news. Yet with limited intellectual bandwidth and financial resources to go around, de-extinction threatens to divert attention from the modern biodiversity crisis. According to a 2012 report from the International Union for Conservation of Nature, some 20,000 species are currently in grave danger of going extinct. Species today are vanishing in such great numbers—many from hunting and habitat destruction—that the trend has been called a sixth mass extinction, an event on par with such die-offs as the one that befell the dinosaurs 65 million years ago. A program to restore extinct species poses a risk of selling the public on a false promise that technology alone can solve our ongoing environmental woes—an implicit assurance that if a species goes away, we can snap our fingers and bring it back.

Already conservationists face difficult choices

about which species and ecosystems to try to save, since they cannot hope to rescue them all. Many countries where poaching and trade in threatened species are rampant either do not want to give up the revenue or lack the wherewithal to enforce their own regulations. Against that backdrop, a costly and flamboyant project to resuscitate extinct flora and fauna in the name of conservation looks irresponsible: Should we resurrect the mammoth only to let elephants go under? Of course not.

That is not to say that the de-extinction enterprise lacks merit altogether. Aspects of it could conceivably help save endangered species. For example, extinct versions of genes could be reintroduced into species and subspecies that have lost a dangerous amount of genetic diversity, such as the black-footed ferret and the northern white rhino. Such investigations, however, should be conducted under the mantle of preserving modern biodiversity rather than conjuring extinct species from the grave.

【Question】

Which choice best states the relationship between the two passages?

A) Passage 2 attacks a political decision that Passage 1 strongly advocates.

B) Passage 2 urges caution regarding a technology that Passage 1 describes in favorable terms.

C) Passage 2 expands on the results of a research study mentioned in Passage 1.

D) Passage 2 considers practical applications that could arise from a theory discussed in Passage 1.

【解析】两篇文章都是讨论 de-extinction 这种技术，可以复活灭绝已久的动物。Passage1 观点是正面的，认为这种技术非常有前景，甚至都不用担心现在濒临灭绝的动物了；Passage2 的主要观点是这种技术转移了我们应该保护动物的注意力，而且由于资金有限，可以复活的动物也是有限的。但是作者是承认这种技术的优势的。

所以两篇文章都认同技术的优点，而第二篇文章同时也指出这种技术不是万能的，不能转移我们的注意力。所以态度是交叉的，答案选择 B—— 第二篇文章对第一篇文章非常赞同的技术持谨慎的态度。

如果态度是部分支持部分反对，通常会使用以下几个词。

- caution (cautious)
- reservation (reserved)
- prudence (prudent)
- warning

练习 1

Passage 1

In a recent survey concerning plagiarism among scholars, two University of Alabama economists asked 1,200 of their colleagues if they believed their work had ever been stolen. A startling 40 percent answered yes. While not a random sample, the responses still represent hundreds of cases of alleged plagiarism. Very few of them will ever be dragged into the sunlight. That is because academia often discourages victims from seeking justice, and when they do, tend to ignore their complaints. "It's like cockroaches," says the author of a recent book about academia fraud. "For every one you see on the floor, there are a hundred behind the stove."

Passage 2

Words belong to the person who wrote them. There are fewer simpler ethical notions than this, particularly as society directs more and more energy toward the creation of intellectual property. In the past 30 years, copyright laws have been strengthened, fighting piracy has become an obsession with Hollywood, and, in the worlds of academia and publishing, plagiarism has gone from being bad literary manners to something close to a felony. When a noted historian was recently found to have lifted passages from other historians, she was asked to resign from the board of the Pulitzer Prize committee. And why not? If she had robbed a bank, she would have been fired the next day.

【Question 1】

Which best expresses the relationship between the two passages?

A) Passage 1 advocates a strategy that Passage 2 criticizes.

B) Passage 1 describes a phenomenon that Passage 2 views as inexcusable.

C) Passage 1 emphasize a problem, and Passage 2 presents its effect.

D) Passage 1 envisions an ideal condition that Passage 2 finds impossible.

【Question 2】

Both passages discuss which of the following?

A) reactions to plagiarism committed by scholars.

B) an increase in plagiarism by college professors.

C) a major change in copyright laws.

D) recent and highly publicized cases of plagiarism.

【解析】两篇文章都是讨论学术剽窃的话题。第一篇文章主要指出这种现象的广泛性以及学术界对于这种现象的忽视甚至是纵容的态度；而第二篇文章强调由于各领域对于知识产权保护意识的增强，学术界对这种事情不能容忍。

第一题：两篇文章关系答案选择 B——第一篇文章描述了一个现象，而第二篇文章觉得这种现象是不可原谅的。A 选项错误，第一篇文章并没有支持任何策略；C 选项错误，第二篇文章的重点不是剽窃的影响，而是人们对待剽窃的态度；D 选项错误，因为第一篇文章没有想象任何理想的情况。

第二题考查两篇文章都在讨论什么话题，答案比较明显，选择 A 选项。两篇文章都在讨论对待学术剽窃的态度（但是态度相反）。

练习 2

Passage 1 is adapted from Talleyrand et al., *Report on Public Instruction*. Originally published in 1791. Passage 2 is adapted from Mary Wollstonecraft, *A Vindication of the Rights of Woman*. Originally published in 1792. Talleyrand was a French diplomat; the *Report* was a plan for national education. Wollstonecraft, a British novelist and political writer, wrote *Vindication* in response to Talleyrand.

Passage 1

That half the human race is excluded by the other half from any participation in government; that they are native by birth but foreign by law in the very land where they were born; and that they are property-owners yet have no direct influence or representation: are all political phenomena apparently impossible to explain on abstract principle. But on another level of ideas, the question changes and may be easily resolved. The purpose of all these institutions must be the happiness of the greatest number. Everything that leads us farther from this purpose is in error; everything that brings us closer is truth. If the exclusion from public employments decreed against women leads to a greater sum of mutual happiness for the two sexes, then this becomes a law that all Societies have been compelled to acknowledge and sanction.

Any other ambition would be a reversal of our primary destinies; and it will never be in women's interest to change the assignment they have received. It seems to us incontestable that our common happiness, above all that of women, requires that they never aspire to the exercise of political rights and functions. Here we must seek their interests in the wishes of nature. Is it not apparent, that their delicate constitutions, their peaceful inclinations, and the many duties of motherhood, set them apart from strenuous habits and onerous duties, and summon them to gentle occupations and the cares of the home? And is it not evident that the great conserving principle of Societies, which makes the division of powers a source of harmony, has been expressed and revealed by nature itself, when it divided the functions of the two sexes in so obviously distinct a manner? This is sufficient; we need not invoke principles that are inapplicable to the question. Let us not make rivals of life's companions. You must, you truly must allow the persistence of a union that no interest, no rivalry, can possibly undo. Understand that the good of all demands this of you.

Passage 2

Contending for the rights of woman, my main argument is built on this simple principle, that if she be not prepared by education to become the companion of man, she will stop the progress of knowledge and virtue; for truth must be common to all, or it will be inefficacious with respect to its influence on general practice. And how can woman be expected to co-operate unless she know why she ought to be virtuous? Unless freedom strengthen her reason till she comprehend her duty, and see in what manner it is connected with her real good? If children are to be educated to understand the true principle of patriotism, their mother must be a patriot; and the love of mankind, from which an orderly train of virtues spring, can only be produced by considering the moral and civil interest of mankind; but the education and situation of woman, at present, shuts her out from such investigations...

Consider, sir, dispassionately, these observations—for a glimpse of this truth seemed to open before you when you observed, "that to see one half of the human race excluded by the other from all participation of government, was a political phenomenon that, according to abstract principles, it was impossible to explain." If so, on what does your constitution rest? If the abstract rights of man will bear discussion and explanation, those of woman, by a parity of reasoning, will not shrink from the same test: though a different opinion prevails in this country, built on the very arguments which you use to justify the oppression of woman—prescription.

Consider—I address you as a legislator—whether, when men contend for their freedom, and to be allowed to judge for themselves respecting their own happiness, it be not inconsistent and unjust to subjugate women, even though you firmly believe that you are acting in the manner best calculated to promote their happiness? Who made man the exclusive judge, if woman partake with him the gift of reason?

In this style, argue tyrants of every denomination, from the weak king to the weak father of a family; they are all eager to crush reason; yet always assert that they usurp its throne only to be useful. Do you not act a similar part, when you force all women, by denying them civil and political rights, to remain immured in their families groping in the dark?

【Question 1】

Which best describes the overall relationship between Passage 1 and Passage 2?

A) Passage 2 strongly challenges the point of view in Passage 1.

B) Passage 2 draws alternative conclusions from the evidence presented in Passage 1.

C) Passage 2 elaborates on the proposal presented in Passage 1.

D) Passage 2 restates in different terms the argument presented in Passage 1

【Question 2】

The authors of both passages would most likely agree with which of the following statements about women in the eighteenth century?

A) Their natural preferences were the same as those of men.

B) They needed a good education to be successful in society.

C) They were just as happy in life as men were.

D) They generally enjoyed fewer rights than men did.

【Question 3】

How would the authors of Passage 1 most likely respond to the points made in the final paragraph of Passage 2?

A) disapproval, because women are not naturally suited for the exercise of civil and political rights.

B) support, because men and women possess similar degrees of reasoning ability.

C) Women do not need to remain confined to their traditional family duties.

D) The principles of natural law should not be invoked when considering gender roles.

【解析】两篇文章的共同话题：女性的权利和社会地位。

第一篇文章的主要观点：女性按照自然分工就是适合从事轻松的工作，照顾家庭，相夫教子，不应该参与政治。

第二篇文章的主要观点：男女平等，女性也应享有追求自己幸福的权利。

所以两篇文章观点冲突类，第一题答案选择 A。

第二题是求同题，问关于 18 世纪的女性，两篇作者都同意的说法是哪一个?

A 选项错误，因为第一篇文章认为按照自然分工两性是不一样的。

B 选项错误，第一篇文章没有涉及教育的内容。

C 选项错误，两篇都没有直接提到女性是否感到幸福。第一篇文章只是说为了女性的幸福，女性应该从事轻松的工作，但是没有提到任何有关幸福的事实。

D 选项正确，因为第一篇文章在开头就提到在当时的社会条件下，女性确实享受到的权利是很少的；第二篇文章也提到了女性应该享有相同的权利，言外之意就是女性在实际生活中没有和男性享有同等的权利。

第三题是观点回应题，问第一篇文章的作者会如何回应第二篇文章的最后一段。对于观点回应题，在解题时可分成三步。

(1) 作者观点判断：第一篇文章认为女性不应该追求政治权利，女性应该照顾家庭，这是自然的安排。

(2) 内容确定：第二篇文章最后一段说的是反对任何暴政，也就是说，女性应该和男性保持平等地位。

(3) 观点和内容的关系，是同意、反对还是混合态度，很明显：第一篇文章作者的观点和第二篇最后一段的内容是相冲突的。所以一定是负面的回应，而原因就是第一篇文章作者的观点。所以这道题答案选择 A。

SAT 重要历史文献与评析

一、《独立宣言》（*The Declaration of Independence*）

> IN CONGRESS, JULY 4, 1776
>
> THE UNANIMOUS DECLARATION OF THE THIRTEEN UNITED STATES OF AMERAICA
>
> When in the course of human events, it becomes necessary for one people to dissolve the political bands which have connected them with another, and to assume among the powers of the earth, the separate and equal station to which the laws of Nature and of Nature's God entitle them, a decent respect to the opinions of mankind requires that they should declare the causes which impel them to the separation.

【评析】开门见山，通过寻找和理解主要句子可以得知《独立宣言》的目的就是为了宣布独立之原因。

> We hold these truths to be self-evident, that all men are created equal, that they are endowed by their creator with certain unalienable rights, that among these are life, liberty and the pursuit of happiness.

【评析】先说天赋人权，注意这里用的是 created equal，也就是说上帝 (the creator) 在创造人类的时候赋予大家平等的地位。此外，生命、自由和追求幸福的权利也是不可剥夺的。而这四个单词——equal、life、liberty 和 happiness 可以说贯穿整个美国历史，也很好地体现在美国各类影视大片中。比如提到 life，我想到了 Tom Hanks 的 *Cast Away*（《荒岛余生》）；比如提到 liberty，我想到了 *The Shawshank Redemption*（《肖申克的救赎》）；比如提到 happiness，直接想到了这部影片——*The Pursuit of Happiness*（《当幸福来敲门》）。

That to secure these rights, governments are instituted among them, deriving their just power from the consent of the governed. That whenever any form of government becomes destructive of these ends, it is the right of the people to alter or to abolish it, and to institute new government, laying its foundation on such principles and organizing its powers in such form, as to them shall seem most likely to effect their safety and happiness.

【评析】转而提到政府的功能——保护大家的权利。让人比较震撼的是在这样一部伟大的宣言中，清晰地表达出对政府的改变或废除的条件：如果政府侵犯大家的权利，人们则有权去改变或是废除政府，然后建立新的政府。

上面两段讲完之后如何回答第一段提到的独立原因呢？我们看看这个逻辑。

人生而平等，且有生命、自由和追求幸福的权利。

政府是保护广大民众权利的；如果民众权利遭侵犯，则可以改变或废除政府。

美国殖民地当时处于英国统治和管辖中。

那么下文只要提到英国政府对殖民地人民的暴力统治，就能形成完整的独立逻辑。所以我们可以合理地预测后文主要列举英国殖民者的各类暴政。

Prudence, indeed, will dictate that governments long established should not be changed for light and transient causes; and accordingly all experience hath shown, that mankind are more disposed to suffer, while evils are sufferable, than to right themselves by abolishing the forms to which they are accustomed. But when a long train of abuses and usurpations, pursuing invariably the same object evinces a design to reduce them under absolute despotism, it is their right, it is their duty, to throw off such government, and to provide new guards for their future security. —Such has been the patient sufferance of these colonies; and such is now the necessity which constrains them to alter their former systems of government. The history of the present King of Great Britain is a history of repeated injuries and usurpations, all having in direct object the establishment of an absolute tyranny over these states. To prove this, let facts be submitted to a candid world.

【评析】引出下文列举的事实。

He has refused his assent to Laws, the most wholesome and necessary for the public good.

He has forbidden his governors to pass laws of immediate and pressing importance, unless suspended in their operation till his assent should be obtained; and when so suspended, he has utterly neglected to attend to them.

He has refused to pass other laws for the accommodation of large districts of people, unless those people would relinquish the right of representation in the Legislature, a right inestimable to them and formidable to tyrants only.

He has called together legislative bodies at places unusual, uncomfortable, and distant from the depository of their public records, for the sole purpose of fatiguing them into compliance with his measures.

He has dissolved Representative Houses repeatedly, for opposing with manly firmness his invasions on the rights of the people.

He has refused for a long time, after such dissolutions, to cause others to be elected; whereby the legislative powers, incapable of annihilation, have returned to the people at large for their exercise; the State remaining in the mean time exposed to all the dangers of invasion from without, and convulsions within.

He has endeavoured to prevent the population of these states; for that purpose obstructing the laws for naturalization of foreigners; refusing to pass others to encourage their migrations hither, and raising the conditions of new appropriations of lands.

He has obstructed the administration of Justice, by refusing his assent to laws for establishing judiciary powers.

He has made judges dependent on his will alone, for the tenure of their offices, and the amount and payment of their salaries.

He has erected a multitude of new offices, and sent hither swarms of officers to harrass our people, and eat out their substance.

He has kept among us, in times of peace, standing armies without the Consent of our legislatures.

He has affected to render the military independent of and superior to the civil power.

He has combined with others to subject us to a jurisdiction foreign to our constitution, and unacknowledged by our laws; giving his assent to their acts of pretended legislation.

For quartering large bodies of armed troops among us.

For protecting them, by a mock trial, from punishment for any murders which they should commit on the inhabitants of these states.

For cutting off our trade with all parts of the world.

For imposing taxes on us without our Consent.

For depriving us in many cases, of the benefits of trial by jury.

For transporting us beyond seas to be tried for pretended offences.

For abolishing the free system of english laws in a neighbouring province, establishing therein an arbitrary government, and enlarging its boundaries so as to render it at once an example and fit instrument for introducing the same absolute rule into these colonies.

For taking away our charters, abolishing our most valuable laws, and altering fundamentally the forms of our governments.

For suspending our own legislatures, and declaring themselves invested with power to legislate for us in all cases whatsoever.

He has abdicated government here, by declaring us out of his protection and waging war against us.

He has plundered our seas, ravaged our coasts, burnt our towns, and destroyed the lives of our people.

He is at this time transporting large armies of foreign mercenaries to complete the works of death, desolation and tyranny, already begun with circumstances of cruelty and perfidy scarcely paralleled in the most barbarous ages, and totally unworthy the head of a civilized nation.

He has constrained our fellow citizens taken captive on the high seas to bear arms against their country, to become the executioners of their friends and brethren, or to fall themselves by their hands.

He has excited domestic insurrections amongst us, and has endeavoured to bring on the inhabitants of our frontiers, the merciless Indian savages, whose known rule of warfare, is an undistinguished destruction of all ages, sexes and conditions.

【评析】到这本列举结束，让世人了解英国国王 / 政府的累累罪行。

In every stage of these oppressions we have petitioned for redress in the most humble terms: Our repeated petitions have been answered only by repeated injury. A prince whose character is thus marked by every act which may define a tyrant, is unfit to be the ruler of a free people.

Nor have we been wanting in attentions to our British brethren. We have warned them from time to time of attempts by their legislature to extend an unwarrantable jurisdiction over us. We have reminded them of the circumstances of our emigration and settlement here. We have appealed to their native justice and magnanimity, and we have conjured them by the ties of our common kindred to disavow these usurpations, which, would inevitably interrupt our connections and correspondence. They too have been deaf to the voice of justice and of consanguinity. We must, therefore, acquiesce in the necessity, which denounces our separation, and hold them, as we hold the rest of mankind, enemies in war, in peace friends.

We, therefore, the representatives of the United States of America, in General Congress, assembled, appealing to the Supreme Judge of the world for the rectitude of our intentions, do, in the name, and by the authority of the good people of these colonies, solemnly publish and declare, That these united colonies are, and of right ought to be free and independent States; that they are absolved from all allegiance to the British Crown, and that all political connection between them and the state of Great Britain, is and ought to be totally dissolved; and that as free and independent states, they have full power to levy war, conclude peace, contract alliances, establish commerce, and to do all other acts and things which independent states may of right do. And for the support of this declaration, with a firm reliance on the protection of divine Providence, we mutually pledge to each other our lives, our fortunes and our sacred honor.

【评析】最后一句呼吁大家支持《独立宣言》，并且为之付出生命。

二、美国联邦宪法（The Constitution of the United States of America）

1. 序言（Preamble）

We the people of the United States, in order to form a more perfect union, establish justice, insure domestic tranquility, provide for the common defence, promote the general welfare, and secure the blessings of liberty to ourselves and our posterity, do ordain and establish this Constitution for the United States of America.

Article I-VII

【评析】在序言之后，美国宪法的正文由 7 个章节组成，主要规定了政府三大权力机构的组织和运作、各州与联邦政府的关系、宪法本身的修改和批准程序等。

美国宪法第一章规定了立法机构即美国国会的权力和组织。美国国会包括众议院和参议院两部分。宪法规定了国会议员的选举办法以及任职资格条件。此外，条文还简要规定了立法程序以及国会的职权范围。第一章的末尾规定了对联邦和各州立法机关的限制。

美国宪法第二章规定了行政机构即美国总统的相关事项：美国总统选举的程序、政府官员任职资格、就任仪式的宣誓、政府官员的权力和职责、指派官员的程序。同时，这一章还特别规定了美国副总统的职位，并规定在美国总统失去行为能力或者辞职之后由副总统继任其职位。宪法规定，美国副总统兼任美国参议院议长一职，但是在近些年来的实践中，这种做法已非常少见。第二章最后还规定了对政府官员（包括总统、副总统、法官和其他官员）的弹劾以及免职程序。

美国宪法第三章是对司法机关即美国联邦法院系统（包括美国联邦最高法院）的有关规定。宪法规定要建立一个最高法院，原则上美国国会可以设立低级别的法院，而所有低级法院的判决和命令都可由最高法院进行再审。这一章还规定了所有刑事诉讼都要实行陪审团制度、叛国罪的定义、国会对于叛国罪的处罚以及限制。

美国宪法第四章规定了各州与联邦政府之间以及各州之间的关系。例如，宪法规定，各州政府要完全尊重和充分信赖其他州的法令、记录和司法程序。国会有权调整各州承认上述文件效力的程序。“特权和免责条款”禁止各州政府为了本地居民利益而差别性地对待其他州的居民。

美国宪法第五章规定了修正美国宪法的程序。早在宪法制定之初，宪法的起草者们就已经清楚地意识到随着国家的发展和时代的变迁，宪法需要不断修改。同时，他们也认为宪法的修改不宜过于频繁。为了做到两者的平衡，起草者们设计了一套启动修宪的双重程序。

美国宪法第六章规定了宪法本身和联邦政府制定的法律以及签订的条约在全国范围内具有最高权威。同时，宪法也确认了根据邦联条例而发行的国债，还要求所有立法、行政、司法机关要宣誓维护宪法的地位。

美国宪法第七章规定了这部宪法本身得以生效的表决程序。起初美国宪法作为邦联条例的修正形式，需要获得全部 13 个州的批准方能生效。然而，宪法第七章只要求获得 9 个州以上的批准就可以使宪法生效。为此，许多学者认为一旦只有 9 个州批准了这部宪法草案，那么将从原有的邦联中脱离出来，成立一个新的联邦体国家。而不批准的其余州将留在旧邦联体制内。事实上，这种理论并没有得到实践的印证，因为 13 个州最终全部批准了这部宪法。

2. 美国宪法的历次修改

截至目前为止，美国宪法共通过了 27 个有效的修正案。其中，最初的 10 个修正案是一次性被通过的，因为其主要规定了人民的权利和对政府的限制，因此被统称为权利法案。此后的 17 个修正案则是逐次获得通过的。

<table>
<tr><th>序号</th><th>日期</th><th>修正案内容</th></tr>
<tr><td rowspan="2">1</td><td>1791年12月15日</td><td>信仰、出版、集会、示威自由</td></tr>
<tr><td colspan="2">Congress shall make no law respecting an establishment of religion, or prohibiting the free exercise thereof; or abridging the freedom of speech, or of the press; or the right of the people peaceably to assemble, and to petition the Government for a redress of grievances.</td></tr>
<tr><td rowspan="2">2</td><td>1791年12月15日</td><td>携带武器的自由</td></tr>
<tr><td colspan="2">A well regulated militia, being necessary to the security of a free state, the right of the people to keep and bear arms, shall not be infringed.</td></tr>
<tr><td rowspan="2">3</td><td>1791年12月15日</td><td>军队不得进入民房</td></tr>
<tr><td colspan="2">No soldier shall, in time of peace be quartered in any house, without the consent of the owner, nor in time of war, but in a manner to be prescribed by law.</td></tr>
<tr><td rowspan="2">4</td><td>1791年12月15日</td><td>免于不合理的搜查与扣押</td></tr>
<tr><td colspan="2">The right of the people to be secure in their persons, houses, papers, and effects, against unreasonable searches and seizures, shall not be violated, and no warrants shall issue, but upon probable cause, supported by oath or affirmation, and particularly describing the place to be searched, and the persons or things to be seized.</td></tr>
<tr><td rowspan="2">5</td><td>1791年12月15日</td><td>正当审判程序、一罪不再理、无罪推定、征用私产需赔偿</td></tr>
<tr><td colspan="2">No person shall be held to answer for a capital, or otherwise infamous crime, unless on a presentment or indictment of a Grand Jury, except in cases arising in the land or naval forces, or in the militia, when in actual service in time of war or public danger; nor shall any person be subject for the same offense to be twice put in jeopardy of life or limb; nor shall be compelled in any criminal case to be a witness against himself, nor be deprived of life, liberty, or property, without due process of law; nor shall private property be taken for public use without just compensation.</td></tr>
<tr><td rowspan="2">6</td><td>1791年12月15日</td><td>刑事案件接受陪审团审判的权利</td></tr>
<tr><td colspan="2">In all criminal prosecutions, the accused shall enjoy the right to a speedy and public trial, by an impartial jury of the State and district wherein the crime shall have been committed, which district shall have been previously ascertained by law, and to be informed of the nature and cause of the accusation; to be confronted with the witnesses against him; to have compulsory process for obtaining witnesses in his favor, and to have the assistance of counsel for his defense.</td></tr>
</table>

<table>
<tr><td rowspan="2">7</td><td>1791 年 12 月 15 日</td><td>民事案件接受陪审团审判的权利</td></tr>
<tr><td colspan="2">In suits at common law, where the value in controversy shall exceed twenty dollars, the right of trial by jury shall be preserved, and no fact tried by a jury shall be otherwise reexamined in any court of the United States, than according to the rules of the common law.</td></tr>
<tr><td rowspan="2">8</td><td>1791 年 12 月 15 日</td><td>禁止过度严厉的刑罚和罚款</td></tr>
<tr><td colspan="2">Excessive bail shall not be required, nor excessive fines imposed, nor cruel and unusual punishments inflicted.</td></tr>
<tr><td rowspan="2">9</td><td>1791 年 12 月 15 日</td><td>宪法未列明的权利同样受保护</td></tr>
<tr><td colspan="2">The enumeration in the Constitution, of certain rights, shall not be construed to deny or disparage others retained by the people.</td></tr>
<tr><td rowspan="2">10</td><td>1791 年 12 月 15 日</td><td>宪法未赋予政府的权利都属于各州和人民</td></tr>
<tr><td colspan="2">The powers not delegated to the United States by the Constitution, nor prohibited by it to the States, are reserved to the States respectively, or to the people.</td></tr>
<tr><td>11</td><td>1795 年 2 月 7 日</td><td>限制联邦法院对各州的管辖权</td></tr>
<tr><td>12</td><td>1804 年 6 月 15</td><td>总统选举办法</td></tr>
<tr><td rowspan="3">13</td><td>1865 年 12 月 6 日</td><td>废除奴隶制度</td></tr>
<tr><td colspan="2">AMENDMENT XIII
Note: A portion of Article IV, section 2, of the Constitution was superseded by the 13th amendment.</td></tr>
<tr><td colspan="2">Section 1. Neither slavery nor involuntary servitude, except as a punishment for crime whereof the party shall have been duly convicted, shall exist within the United States, or any place subject to their jurisdiction.
Section 2. Congress shall have power to enforce this article by appropriate legislation.</td></tr>
<tr><td>14</td><td>1868 年 7 月 9 日</td><td>国籍、处罚程序、众议员选举、叛国罪、国债，所有公民享有平等被保护权</td></tr>
<tr><td rowspan="2">15</td><td>1870 年 2 月 3 日</td><td>所有公民不得由于肤色和种族的区别而受到选举权的限制（不包括性别）。</td></tr>
<tr><td colspan="2">AMENDMENT XV
Passed by Congress February 26, 1869. Ratified February 3, 1870.
Section 1. The right of citizens of the United States to vote shall not be denied or abridged by the United States or by any State on account of race, color, or previous condition of servitude.
Section 2. The Congress shall have the power to enforce this article by appropriate legislation.</td></tr>
</table>

16	1913 年 2 月 3 日	国会对所得税的征收权
17	1913 年 4 月 8 日	代表各州的联邦参议员必须直接选举
18	1919 年 1 月 16 日	禁止在美国国内制造、运输酒类（后被第 21 条废止）
19	1920 年 8 月 18 日	禁止选举中的性别歧视
	AMENDMENT XIX Passed by Congress June 4, 1919. Ratified August 18, 1920. The right of citizens of the United States to vote shall not be denied or abridged by the United States or by any State on account of sex. Congress shall have power to enforce this article by appropriate legislation.	
20	1933 年 1 月 23 日	规定总统任期、国会议事程序
21	1933 年 12 月 5 日	废除第 18 条修正案
22	1951 年 2 月 27 日	总统最多连任一次
23	1961 年 3 月 19 日	首都华盛顿哥伦比亚特区的选举规则
24	1964 年 1 月 23 日	选举权不受税收限制
25	1967 年 2 月 10 日	总统与副总统的继任规则
26	1971 年 7 月 1 日	保护 18 岁以上公民选举权
27	1992 年 5 月 7 日	禁止随意改动议员薪酬

三、《乔治·华盛顿告别演说》(*Farewell Address by Gorge Washington*)（节选）

Friends and Citizens:

The period for a new election of a citizen to administer the executive government of the United States being not far distant, and the time actually arrived when your thoughts must be employed in designating the person who is to be clothed with that important trust, it appears to me proper, especially as it may conduce to a more distinct expression of the public voice, that I should now apprise you of the resolution I have formed, to decline being considered among the number of those out of whom a choice is to be made.

【评析】乔治•华盛顿，美国首任总统，被称为国父，美国独立战争大陆军总司令。1789 年，他经过全体选举团无异议的支持而成为美国第一任总统，在接连两次选举中都获得了全体选举团无异议支持，一直担任总统直到 1797 年。

而从这段话中可以看到华盛顿对权力的淡泊，担任两届总统之后则明确表示拒绝再次出任总统。

I beg you, at the same time, to do me the justice to be assured that this resolution has not been taken without a strict regard to all the considerations appertaining to the relation which binds a dutiful citizen to his country; and that in withdrawing the tender of service, which silence in my situation might imply, I am influenced by no diminution of zeal for your future interest, no deficiency of grateful respect for your past kindness, but am supported by a full conviction that the step is compatible with both.

【评析】此段说明华盛顿不想继续担任总统的原因，完全是为了国家的将来以及对大家的尊重。

……

The unity of government which constitutes you one people is also now dear to you. It is justly so, for it is a main pillar in the edifice of your real independence, the support of your tranquility at home, your peace abroad; of your safety; of your prosperity; of that very liberty which you so highly prize. But as it is easy to foresee that, from different causes and from different quarters, much pains will be taken, many artifices employed to weaken in your minds the conviction of this truth; as this is the point in your political fortress against which the batteries of internal and external enemies will be most constantly and actively (though often covertly and insidiously) directed, it is of infinite moment that you should properly estimate the immense value of your national union to your collective and individual happiness; that you should cherish a cordial, habitual, and immovable attachment to it; accustoming yourselves to think and speak of it as of the palladium of your political safety and prosperity; watching for its preservation with jealous anxiety; discountenancing whatever may suggest even a suspicion that it can in any event be abandoned; and indignantly frowning upon the first dawning of every attempt to alienate any portion of our country from the rest, or to enfeeble the sacred ties which now link together the various parts.

【评析】在这个段落，华盛顿就国家统一表达自己的看法：国家的统一和联合是异常珍贵的，是国家和人民独立的支柱，是国内安宁和人民安全的保障。由此可知，在 SAT 常考的联邦邦联话题中，华盛顿是支持联邦制度的。

For this you have every inducement of sympathy and interest. Citizens, by birth or choice, of a common country, that country has a right to concentrate your affections. The name of American, which belongs to you in your national capacity, must always exalt the just pride of patriotism more than any appellation derived from local discriminations. With slight shades of difference, you have the same religion, manners, habits, and political principles. You have in a common cause fought and triumphed together; the independence and liberty you possess are the work of joint counsels, and joint efforts of common dangers, sufferings, and successes…

【评析】再次强调美国人民的共同情感和利益。大家务必众志成城，抵御潜在危险和威胁。

四、七月四号对奴隶来说是什么（What to the Slave is the Fourth of July?）

Frederick Douglass

July 5, 1852

【评析】弗雷德里克·道格拉斯，19 世纪美国废奴运动领袖，母亲是一个黑人奴隶，父亲是一个白人。道格拉斯是一名杰出的演说家、作家、人道主义者和政治活动家。在废奴运动中，他具有举足轻重的作用。

这篇演讲发表于 1852 年 7 月 5 日，道格拉斯受邀去纽约州罗切斯特做演讲。这篇演讲的目的是让大家去接受在当时还未被广泛认可的废奴主义运动。同时，他想改变大家对黑人的偏见看法，想证明黑人也是一样富有智力和能力的。

……

Fellow-citizens, pardon me, allow me to ask, why am I called upon to speak here to-day? What have I, or those I represent, to do with your national independence? Are the great principles of political freedom and of natural justice, embodied in that Declaration of Independence, extended to us? and am I, therefore, called upon to bring our humble offering to the national altar, and to confess the benefits and express devout gratitude for the blessings resulting from your independence to us?

【评析】这个段落全部是问句：一是为了激起大家的思考；二是想强调黑人在当时并未享受到美国独立所获得的公正。

Would to God, both for your sakes and ours, that an affirmative answer could be truthfully returned to these questions! Then would my task be light, and my burden easy and delightful. For who is there so cold, that a nation's sympathy could not warm him? Who so obdurate and dead to the claims of gratitude, that would not thankfully acknowledge such priceless benefits? Who so stolid and selfish, that would not give his voice to swell the hallelujahs of a nation's jubilee, when the chains of servitude had been torn from his limbs? I am not that man. In a case like that, the dumb might eloquently speak, and the "lame man leap as an hart."

【评析】本段开头以虚拟语气说明上面段落中的问题并没有肯定的答案，后面仍然以排比的手法说明只要黑人也享有权利和公正，肯定会对美国感恩戴德的。

But, such is not the state of the case. I say it with a sad sense of the disparity between us. I am not included within the pale of this glorious anniversary! Your high independence only reveals the immeasurable distance between us. The blessings in which you, this day, rejoice, are not enjoyed in common. — The rich inheritance of justice, liberty, prosperity and independence, bequeathed by your fathers, is shared by you, not by me. The sunlight that brought life and healing to you, has brought stripes and death to me. This Fourth [of] July is yours, not mine. You may rejoice, I must mourn. To drag a man in fetters into the grand illuminated temple of liberty, and call upon him to join you in joyous anthems, were inhuman mockery and sacrilegious irony.

【评析】本段强调了黑人和白人之间的巨大差异。白人享受独立，黑人仍然困于奴役之中。

……

What, am I to argue that it is wrong to make men brutes, to rob them of their liberty, to work them without wages, to keep them ignorant of their relations to their fellow men, to beat them with sticks, to flay their flesh with the lash, to load their limbs with irons, to hunt them with dogs, to sell them at auction, to sunder their families, to knock out their teeth, to burn their flesh, to starve them into obedience and submission to their masters? Must I argue that a system thus marked with blood, and stained with pollution, is wrong? No! I will not. I have better employments for my time and strength than such arguments would imply.

【评析】本段以排比的写作手法说明黑人遭受的种种不公和磨难，同时能够感受到道格拉斯演讲时的愤怒情感。

What, then, remains to be argued? Is it that slavery is not divine; that God did not establish it; that our doctors of divinity are mistaken? There is blasphemy in the thought. That which is inhuman, cannot be divine! Who can reason on such a proposition? They that can, may; I cannot. The time for such argument is passed.

【评析】强调奴隶制并非是上帝的旨意，它是不公正的。

五、《感伤宣言》(*The Declaration of Sentiments*)

这份文档是 1848 年在纽约 Seneca Falls 由 100 位参与者共同签署的关于女性权利的重要文献。文档的主要作者是 Elizabeth Cady Stanton；她基本上是模仿《独立宣言》的结构来完成这篇文档的。所以无论是开头句，还是第二段提到的真理，大家都能感受到《独立宣言》的意味。

> When, in the course of human events, it becomes necessary for one portion of the family of man to assume among the people of the earth a position different from that which they have hitherto occupied, but one to which the laws of nature and of nature's God entitle them, a decent respect to the opinions of mankind requires that they should declare the causes that impel them to such a course.

【评析】开头段是长句，理解时候找主干：a decent respect to the opinions of mankind requires that they should declare the causes. 也就是说，女性必须宣布原因(想获得独立平等地位的原因)。这也是这篇文章的目的，宣布一个事情的原因。

> We hold these truths to be self-evident: that all men and women are created equal; that they are endowed by their Creator with certain inalienable rights; that among these are life, liberty, and the pursuit of happiness;

【评析】大家能看出这个段落和《独立宣言》的区别么？对的，只多了两个单词——and women，其他和《独立宣言》一字不差。

这段主要目的就是说明人生而平等。当然，在《独立宣言》中是想说明不同种族或是地方的人民平等，美洲人民不应该受到英国的统治；这里是想说明不同性别的人也是平等的。

> that to secure these rights governments are instituted, deriving their just powers from the consent of the governed. Whenever any form of government becomes destructive of these ends, it is the right of those who suffer from it to refuse allegiance to it, and to insist upon the institution of a new government, laying its foundation on such principles, and organizing its powers in such form, as to them shall seem most likely to effect their safety and happiness.

【评析】此段说明政府的作用以及人民对政府的监督甚至是改变和废除的权力。

Prudence, indeed, will dictate that governments long established should not be changed for light and transient causes; and accordingly all experience hath shown that mankind are more disposed to suffer. while evils are sufferable, than to right themselves by abolishing the forms to which they are accustomed. But when a long train of abuses and usurpations, pursuing invariably the same object, evinces a design to reduce them under absolute despotism, it is their duty to throw off such government, and to provide new guards for their future security. Such has been the patient sufferance of the women under this government, and such is now the necessity which constrains them to demand the equal station to which they are entitled.

The history of mankind is a history of repeated injuries and usurpations on the part of man toward woman, having in direct object the establishment of an absolute tyranny over her. To prove this, let facts be submitted to a candid world.

【评析】下面段落开始列举男性对女性的种种不公平对待。

He has never permitted her to exercise her inalienable right to the elective franchise.

He has compelled her to submit to laws, in the formation of which she had no voice.

He has withheld from her rights which are given to the most ignorant and degraded men--both natives and foreigners.

Having deprived her of this first right of a citizen, the elective franchise, thereby leaving her without representation in the halls of legislation, he has oppressed her on all sides.

He has made her, if married, in the eye of the law, civilly dead.

He has taken from her all right in property, even to the wages she earns.

He has made her, morally, an irresponsible being, as she can commit many crimes with impunity, provided they be done in the presence of her husband. In the covenant of marriage, she is compelled to promise obedience to her husband, he becoming, to all intents and purposes, her master--the law giving him power to deprive her of her liberty, and to administer chastisement.

He has so framed the laws of divorce, as to what shall be the proper causes, and in case of separation, to whom the guardianship of the children shall be given, as to be wholly regardles of the happiness of women--the law, in all cases, going upon a flase supposition of the supremacy of man, and giving all power into his hands.

After depriving her of all rights as a married woman, if single, and the owner of property, he has taxed her to support a government which recognizes her only when her property can be made profitable to it.

He has monopolized nearly all the profitable employments, and from those she is permitted to follow, she receives but a scanty remuneration. He closes against her all the avenues to wealth and distinction which he considers most homorable to himself. As a teacher of theoloy, medicine, or law, she is not known.

He has denied her the facilities for obtaining a thorough education, all colleges being closed against her.

He allows her in church, as well as state, but a subordinate position, claiming apostolic authority for her exclusion from the ministry, and, with some exceptions, from any public participation in the affairs of the church.

He has created a false public sentiment by giving to the world a different code of morals for men and women, by which moral delinquencies which exclude women from society, are not only tolerated, but deemed of little account in man.

He has usurped the prerogative of Jehovah himself, claiming it as his right to assign for her a sphere of action, when that belongs to her conscience and to her God.

He has endeavored, in every way that he could, to destroy her confidence in her own powers, to lessen her self-respect, and to make her willing to lead a dependent and abject life.

Now, in view of this entire disfranchisement of one-half the people of this country, their social and religious degradation--in view of the unjust laws above mentioned, and because women do feel themselves aggrieved, oppressed, and fraudulently deprived of their most sacred rights, we insist that they have immediate admission to all the rights and privileges which belong to them as citizens of the United States.

【评析】最后一段强调参会人员坚持认为女性应享有作为美国公民的所有权利。

图书在版编目（C I P）数据

SAT阅读进阶攻略 / 周日进编著. —北京：中国人民大学出版社，2019.2

ISBN 978-7-300-26257-4

Ⅰ. ①S… Ⅱ. ①周… Ⅲ. ①英语-阅读教学-高等院校-入学考试-美国-自学参考资料 Ⅳ. ①H319.37

中国版本图书馆CIP数据核字（2018）第216224号

SAT阅读进阶攻略

周日进 编著

SAT Yuedu Jinjie Gonglüe

出版发行	中国人民大学出版社		
社 址	北京中关村大街31号	**邮政编码**	100080
电 话	010-62511242（总编室）		010-62511770（质管部）
	010-82501766（邮购部）		010-62514148（门市部）
	010-62515195（发行公司）		010-62515275（盗版举报）
网 址	http://www.crup.com.cn		
	http://www.1kao.com.cn（中国1考网）		
经 销	新华书店		
印 刷	北京昌联印刷有限公司		
规 格	185mm×260mm 16开本	**版 次**	2019年2月第1版
印 张	14 .25	**印 次**	2019年2月第1次印刷
字 数	319 000	**定 价**	38.00元